Swimming with Trout

CHAD HANSON

UNIVERSITY OF NEW MEXICO PRESS ■ ALBUQUERQUE

12 11 10 09 08 07   1 2 3 4 5 6

LIBRARY OF CONGRESS CATALOGING-IN-PUBLICATION DATA

Hanson, Chad, 1969–
Swimming with trout / Chad Hanson.
p. cm.
ISBN 978-0-8263-4184-6 (cloth : alk. paper)
1. Trout fishing—United States.
2. Fly fishing—United States.
3. Hanson, Chad, 1969– I. Title.
SH688.U6H36 2007
799.12'4—dc22
2007017836

DESIGN AND COMPOSITION: *Mina Yamashita*

For Lynn

Contents

Acknowledgments

G rateful acknowledgment is due the editors of the following periodicals, where several of these stories appeared for the first time: *Third Coast*, *Pilgrimage*, *Talking River*, *Big Sky Journal*, *Mountain Gazette*, *South Dakota Review*, *Yale Angler's Journal*, and *North Dakota Quarterly*.

Fly Casting with Crazy Horse

Casper, Wyoming, is Crazy Horse country. This spot on the North Platte River was called Fort Caspar in the 1800s, and it sat square in the middle of the region roamed by the Oglala Sioux. I'm confident I've stood on the same dirt, beside the same streams, and under the same trees that Crazy Horse stood beneath—we have the land in common—but in some ways my world couldn't be more different than the one he knew.

Crazy Horse was a buffalo hunter. In the age when he walked this Earth, the North American bison herds were like the essence of the continent, thundering over the plains. Crazy Horse hunted bison religiously, but for obvious reasons there was never much chance of me becoming a buffalo hunter. I became the next best thing, however. I became a fly-fisher for trout.

Crazy Horse flung arrows at bison. I fling flies at fish. But I suspect if he were alive today, absent any buffalo to hunt, Crazy Horse would be a fly-fisherman. Bison embodied the spirit of the American West, nothing will ever replace them, but trout fill part of the void we created when we drove buffalo to the brink of extinction. Trout prefer high elevation, and they swim in clear running water, one of the last remnants of the West before it was tamed.

Crazy Horse and I have something else in common. He was, and I am, confused and frustrated by the ways of white people. His values were commonly challenged by those of the settlers moving across his country, and my interests are regularly thwarted by the great white engineers' management of Wyoming's waterways. For instance, the water level of the present day North Platte River is determined by the whims of agribusiness. The river's rate of flow is set according to the desires of farmers and ranchers in adjacent states such as Nebraska. One day the Platte can be shallow and clear, then the next it's deep and green; a regional ribbon of split-pea soup.

On pea-soup days the fishing isn't great, each cast brings back a fly covered by a sizable lump of algae. For that reason, in the spring of 2002, I decided to do what Crazy Horse did when he was disconcerted. He went north to get away from the cavalry and Fort Caspar. He made camp on the remote creeks that drain the Bighorn Mountains. In May, with the North Platte gushing green, I decided to trace his footsteps.

In the last four years I've read many books about the man. Among the best are Mari Sandoz's *Crazy Horse: Strange Man of the Oglalas*, Stephen Ambrose's *Crazy Horse and Custer*, and Larry McMurtry's biography simply called *Crazy Horse*. Armed with a record of the great Sioux warrior's favorite places, I drove north out of Casper and across the Montana state line, toward the top of the Bighorn Mountain Range, to a spot where a brook called Shade Creek meanders down out of the high country before it spills onto the plains.

The trip was partly historical. I hoped to build a sense of what the West was like in the time of the Sioux, but it was no accident that the location and topography of the creek suggested trout. I had a lightweight fly rod packed before I settled on a pair of shoes.

Shade Creek is tough to find. That's probably one of the things Crazy Horse liked about it. A web of jeep roads and goat paths coat the Bighorns today, to the point where they act as a labyrinth. In addition, tall bluffs and deep valleys make it hard to survey the area from a practical vantage point, but despite the obstacles, I found my way to the rim of Shade Creek Canyon. I couldn't see the water from where I stood. Still, my map suggested I was in the right place, and something in my gut confirmed it. I set up camp on the canyon rim and packed for a hike down to the brook.

From the beginning, I realized that the cliff near my campsite was not going to work as a route to the water. It was clear that I had to find a wash or a tributary, one that cut to the bottom of the canyon at an angle I could handle without climbing gear. A hundred yards upstream, I found a dry streambed that looked promising. I spent a moment inspecting the path and then started down the dry wash toward Shade Creek.

The hike seemed innocent at first. The trail was easy to follow, but less than a mile along the walls closed in and the sandy lane turned into a cataclysm of boulders. The path disappeared, and I was left to pluck my way down a steep barricade of rubble. Forward progress was taxing, and it was made even tougher by the fact that I was struck by a strange feeling as I climbed through the loose rock lying between the canyon walls.

I am not a member of the quartz crystal and patchouli incense crowd. I do not believe in ghosts, auras, or past lives. I haven't read a single book by Shirley MacLaine, and I don't celebrate the seasonal solstices. I bought a pair of Birkenstock sandals in the eighties, but that's as far as I've dipped into the subculture of the "New Age." I'm a scientist by training, a sociologist by degree. I'm a pragmatist and a bit of a skeptic. That said, there was fear in the canyon. I was moving slowly, but my heart started to gallop as if I were running from a threat. Beads of sweat began to bloom along my hairline despite a chill in the air, and I was struck by a feeling, a presence that's hard to explain.

There were desperate times for the Sioux in the 1860s. Crazy Horse and Sitting Bull had rejected the government's policies, and they flat out refused to camp close to the forts established by whites on Indian land. Instead, they chose to live the old life, far away from the soldiers and settlers. Thus, Crazy Horse and his people were labeled "hostile." That meant they were denied trade, separated from family members who lived near the forts, and hunted down like so many quail.

Even though Crazy Horse was a tower of strength in those times, some members of his tribe were unwilling to stay the course. Some reached the point where they were unwilling to spend another day hiding in canyons, running from the cavalry. In fact, several groups made attempts to leave Crazy Horse's camp in 1867. Small bands tried to make their way south to one of the forts along the North Platte River in order to surrender, but more often than not the groups encountered enemy scouts or armed divisions on the way. The soldiers didn't ask them about their intentions. They gave chase, and if the Sioux were caught, the consequences were grave.

As I wound down the dry wash toward Shade Creek, I passed a number of chasms and crevices that looked like hiding places, and in each dark space I saw women and children huddled together, waiting and hoping to be delivered back to Crazy Horse, to the safety of numbers and the shelter of friends and relatives. At one point, I reached a place where the canyon wall on my left was cleft by a cave that fell away from the streambed. Compelled by a sense of tragedy rising from the shadowy hole in the wall, I stepped in, and the sunlight faded. I pressed my hand through the darkness, lost sight of my fingertips, and the image of a Sioux warrior began to shine.

Was my reading of history playing tricks with my vision? I suppose. Do our minds conjure images that match our understanding of the past when we find ourselves in places with historical significance? Evidently. Are there spirits that still linger in spots where the human drama once played out in a fashion that's hard for us moderns to imagine? It felt that way. And when I reached the bottom of the canyon, I was given another reminder that there might be something out there beyond sensory experience.

deep at the bottom of the thin canals carved in the stream-bed. I thought, "If I were a trout, this would be my house." I drifted my flies over the underwater avenue nearest to me, and I watched a ten-inch silver form rise from the bottom. It was a rainbow, and he'd fallen for the Adams.

The trout flew out of the creek. He dove back down in the channel. He shook his head back and forth, jumped again, made one last run, and then he tuckered out. He gave in to the pull of the line, and he was mine. I held onto the fish for a moment. I admired his green back, black spots, and shimmering rose-colored sides. I looked into his eye—a dark marble with gold-leaf trim, a collector of visions and a symbol of the trout's incorrigible life. Back in the creek he went. I closed my eyes as the trout disappeared below the surface, and the sound of rushing water became a drumbeat of bison hooves.

Depending on the current, rocks on the bottom of Shade Creek are visible to about six feet; however, on my hike upstream I found a pool that stretched the stream's limit of visibility. It was deep. I couldn't tell exactly how far the bottom fell, but it was obviously deeper than anything I fished all day. I figured this might be one of those places where a small creek hides a big fish. I imagined a wise old grandfather trout at the bottom, sucking up bugs year in and year out, growing to a size disproportionate to his surroundings. I tied on a twelve-foot leader, added some weight to the line, and tossed a nymph up near the top of the run. Down it went. The bug dropped slowly out of sight.

Seven seconds later, the pool erupted in a flash of silver. Then the flash turned into a full side view of the chrome and crimson monster at the bottom. He was long—longer than a fish should be in a place like Shade Creek. I held on tight, but after the opening explosion, the oversized trout made a turn. My line went slack and my rod stood still. The cunning fish was gone.

I've been back to the same spot several times in the years since. I can't stay away. There's an image of the wily trout at the bottom of the pool sketched in my memory, and the picture is unforgettable.

Some say the Sioux will never occupy or control their land again, but I'm beginning to believe they'll always haunt the eastern Rockies and the short-grass plains. By the end of the day, I became convinced that their spirits linger in the canyons and remain along the creeks that played host to their camps in the Bighorn Range, and if my experience is an indication of what it's like to feel the recurring presence of Crazy Horse, I want to be haunted by his ghost incessantly.

A Sharp Reminder

Our house is perched six blocks from the North Platte River, nine miles from some of the best trout fishing in the West, and ten minutes from the top of a mountain that begs to be hiked. We're surrounded by ski trails, too. We're lucky. We have enough regular recreation in our lives that a full week or two away from the house hardly ever seems necessary. Still, my wife Lynn believes, despite our outdoor assets, we are lacking in the areas of culture and cuisine, so in order to compensate we set out on a tour of the northern Rockies. We planned to have our fill of art, music, and reasonably fine food, but we agreed to camp on a few of the nights, and I figured I could fly-fish, too.

On a typical sun-drenched morning in August, we drove north out of Casper, headed west at Billings, and made it all the way to Bozeman on day one—even though I insisted that we stop at all of the historical sites with ads along the freeway. I couldn't help myself. Places like the Little Bighorn battle site had been on my list of "must see" spots for years. I felt compelled to walk the hills where Crazy Horse pushed Custer to the brink.

To balance my obsession with history, Lynn found the hippest coffeehouse in every town we passed through. The cafe walls were often lined with contemporary art, some of which looked suspiciously like the finger painting I did as a child, but the mochas and lattes were good and the caffeine fueled the commentary back on the road. Driving down the interstate, wired to the gills, we jabbered like restless monkeys.

We set a swift pace in the beginning, because we had tickets for a concert in Missoula on day two. We had plans to hear a songwriter from the seventies by the name of Steve Forbert. Forbert is famous for the lines, "Meet me in the middle of the day/let me hear you say everything's OK/bring me Southern kisses from your room." Unfortunately, those are the only lines he's famous for. He had a long and productive career, but it was spent in relative obscurity. Forbert's lack of popularity is completely lost on Lynn, however. She's been a diehard fan for years.

After the concert, we retired to the Travelodge, and in the morning we agreed to take our time driving home. We planned to camp and fish our way back, in between espresso stops and field trips. It was easy to do. The days flew by like magpies. We found creeks to camp on every night. Twice we were all alone in the wilderness. We slept in Forest Service campgrounds three different times, but even when we camped in designated sites we had the grounds to ourselves. I don't think there's any question that Americans are loving the West to death, but if you're willing to walk a little bit and pitch a tent, you can still find solitude.

Back in Wyoming, we wound through Yellowstone in awe of the geology. We climbed over the Absaroka Mountains on

Beartooth Pass. We discovered Red Lodge, Montana, spent a day at the Buffalo Bill Historical Center in Cody, and then made a run across the dry, sage-covered plains. We were headed for the Bighorn Mountains.

The "Horns" are my favorite range. They're not jagged like the Tetons or the Wind Rivers. They're not as tall as the peaks in Utah or Colorado. They don't have the personality associated with the San Juans or the Wasatch front, but there is something about them. They pull on me. Even a long way from the Horns, I feel their gravity.

By the time we started climbing out of the Bighorn basin and up into the surrounding hills we were looking for a spot to spend the night. We rolled off the pavement at the sight of an unmarked dirt road that skittered to the left, because we had a hunch it might be hiding a stream, and we were right. We bounded down a short, steep trail and found a brook at the bottom of the hill. With the map, I determined it was Rock Creek.

Rock Creek runs close to the highway, but the path we were on looked deserted. At some point, it might have been a common place for people to cross the stream. There was a unique bridge on the road, 1930s vintage, likely the work of the Civilian Conservation Corps. Over time, it weakened and wore to the point that it could no longer carry cars. It's closed today. But the Forest Service posted a sign near the bridge that urged hikers to cross.

This was the invitation we were looking for. Lynn and I are always glad to leave the car behind. We found a camping spot on the other side of the creek and hauled our gear to the site: tent, stove, lantern, sleeping bags, wine.

By the time we settled in, it was getting late. The air was calm, the sun was sinking, and we were in the midst of what could be called a "Russell Chatham evening." The dusk was so serene, the scene started to resemble one of Chatham's western landscape paintings. Colors became deeper and more perceptible—tree leaves, flower petals, tiny stones on the beach beside the stream. A gentle haze entered in the distance, sharpening our focus on the world in front of us.

I felt the need to go fishing. We were near the end of our trip, and if I had been keeping track, the marks lined up under "lattes sipped" would have been longer than the line under "fish caught." Rock Creek was all I had left.

I saw trout shadows shifting back and forth in the current while we were pitching the tent, so I knew there was a possibility I could redeem myself on Rock Creek, but I didn't have time for any streamside entomology. I tied on a Pale Evening Dun and added a Pheasant Tail Nymph.

The creek was fast and shallow on the whole, but the seasonal cycle of high and low water left a number of quiet pools off to the side, perfect hiding spots for hungry but apprehensive trout. I lofted the Dun up to the top of the run closest to our campsite, and before the fly started drifting, a baby brown slurped it off the surface. We were both startled. I wasn't used to catching fish on my first cast, and he was clearly not accustomed to being caught.

I spent a moment coaxing the trout to shore and then brought him to hand. He was a butter-blond nine-inch brown. I hollered at Lynn back in camp. Since she knows what I've spent on fishing gear over the years, I realized a fish like this probably looked like a small prize, but she also knows it's the width of my smile, not the length of the fish that matters. She doesn't understand my obsession, but she's willing to let me feed it, and I suppose that's all a guy can ask.

I moved upstream stalking pools in succession. The Pheasant Tail Nymph was a hit. I took two more browns and a brook trout. None of the fish were large, but they were feisty and they looked fine against the backdrop of clear water rolling over multicolored rocks—gray, green, yellow, and maroon. I lost track of time while I watched the creek, but the clang of stainless steel pots and pans reminded me that dinner would be ready soon. I had just enough time to try casting under the bridge.

The bridge across Rock Creek is a wonder of engineering. The footings are nothing more than boulders strewn across the stream in their natural state. To achieve proper support for the wooden beams that stretch from one side to the other, the Conservation Corps added smaller stones and mortar to the tops of the creek's tallest rocks. The wooden beams have all gone soft, but the underlying structure is still sound. It's beautiful in the way that good architecture pleases the eye. Even better, for my sake, the bridge creates two deep pools with what amounts to a roof over the top.

The Corps unwittingly built a resort hotel for trout.

I hiked thirty yards downstream and then worked my way up close enough to cast a fly onto the first pool. No luck. I tried the same thing four more times—still nothing. I moved to the second pool, but my fortune didn't improve. On my last cast before dinner, the fly fell softly on the surface, but my line was caught in the current and the bug was pulled across the pool so fast it left a wake. I started reeling in. I was ready for a hot meal and a glass of Johannisberg Riesling, but I would have to wait. In the moment that followed, something unusual happened.

My mind and instincts packed up and headed home, but my hand was still taking up line, and I found myself wrestling with a fish. He wasn't big. He was a brookie about the same size as the others, but there was something odd about the way he tugged and twisted. He was tired from the start. He barely put up a fight.

Then I noticed that he was trailing my Pheasant Tail Nymph by a distance of around seven feet. Did I tie on a third fly? How could this be? Did I add an extra dropper in an unknowing stupor of some kind?

Halfway through the conundrum, it started to look like my nymph had snared the end of a pretied tippet, the kind they sell at bait shops and department stores. It seemed my fly had inadvertently snagged the end of a leader left in the fish's mouth by somebody else. I brought the brookie up to where I could grab him, and that confirmed it: the fish had someone else's fly in his throat.

I tried to pry it loose, but the process of plying the hook only made things worse. If the fly came out, it would cost the brookie his life. I started feeling lousy. I was struck by the unique sense of dread that grabs you when there's a fish—that you didn't mean to harm—dying in your hands. I thought about bapping the trout over the head and leaving him on the bank. I figured he'd make a good meal for an owl or an otter. I thought that might be the merciful, and maybe the responsible thing to do.

Then I remembered a report I read suggesting that lures eventually rust and disappear, leaving foul-hooked fish alive and healthy. I'm not sure if it was the right course of action, but in my moment of ethical impasse, I snipped the line so he didn't have to drag it around, then set him back in the water and watched him swim away.

Is he suffering to this day? I can't say. Is he dead? I'm not sure. If he died, was the death merciful? I don't know the answers to questions like that. But I am still bothered by the feeling that struck me when I pulled the fish from the stream with another man's line jutting out of his mouth, a cold steel hook stuck in his throat.

I didn't feel like part of nature at that moment. In that instant, I felt more like a member of society. Worse, I felt like a consumer. On my walk back to camp, I started thinking about all the places we passed through on our tour: Ennis, Cody, Missoula, Livingston, West Yellowstone. We found fly shops and guide services in every town we passed through with populations of more than fifty. I'm telling you—Americans have gone trout mad.

There was a time when fly-fishing was a ritual practiced by an elite band of eccentrics, casting hand-tied flies to unsuspecting trout. Today, fly-fishing is more than anyone imagined it could be. It's a multimillion-dollar sector of the global economy, and despite being damned enjoyable, it's a big money-guzzling industry. I sulked back to camp with my heart in my shoes. I felt like a cog in the machine—one more card-carrying member of the hook-casting hordes that flail away at western streams.

I started struggling with an old question, "Why *do* I fly-fish for trout?" I've faced the issue before, although this was the first time I ever confronted the subject on my own. In the past, the question had always been posed by one of the animal-rights types I knew in college. Some of them couldn't understand why a person would willfully pierce the lip of a fellow creature, drag her through the water for who knows how long, just to turn around and let her go again.

For the self-ordained defenders of fish that I knew in college, I always had an answer. I'd say, "I put a serious tear in my lip once. I know what it feels like. It doesn't hurt. It's uncomfortable . . . I wouldn't recommend it . . . but it isn't painful." Then I'd raise the right side of my mustache to reveal the place where it took fourteen stitches to put my mouth back together after a jagged rock split my lip in two at the end of a tumble I took off the side of a cliff on a mountain bike. I've never been caught in the sense that fish are caught; I just fell off my bike at a bad time. Still, the scar always ensured an end to the discussion. The mark I wear on my lip appears like an odd credential, somehow granting me the privilege to fish, at least in conversations with animal-rights activists.

But this was me I was talking to. The "I've been through it myself" story was old news, and it didn't satisfy my interest in an explanation of the forces that drive me to fly-fish. Having just released a brookie back into a stream with someone else's hook in his mouth, I was looking for more than justification. I wanted a genuine explanation of the forces that push me toward rivers and streams, fly rod in hand, over and over again, year in and year out.

I puzzled my way through dinner. Lynn knew something was wrong so she asked, and I told her about my quandary. She understood the question, but she couldn't come up with a good explanation for why I fish. It turns out she asks herself why I fly-fish every time I come home from the tackle shop with a new gizmo, and knowing that didn't help. I fell asleep wondering whether I'd go on fishing for trout.

We broke camp in the morning. We were almost out of vacation days and we weren't too far from the house. One more leisurely mountain drive and we'd be back to our home and our lives. We climbed in the truck after a cup of coffee and continued up the western flank of the Bighorns. It was a memorable trip. We saw six moose grazing in a swamp on the side of the road. We passed rocky peaks, lush meadows, and tall pine forests. We drove by a sign for a campground that looked enticing, and I pleaded with Lynn, "Can we check it out?"

She gave in, and we found the campground at the end of a long gravel road. The grounds were unremarkable, typical Forest Service fare, but the site was adjacent to a high mountain meadow with a stream winding through the middle and dime-sized flowers all around. I popped out of the car and walked out toward the water without saying a word. After a moment, I crowed, "Let me take a look at this creek." Lynn rolled down her window and shot back a long "Heeeeey." She knew this could lead to an all-day expedition, so I consoled her by adding, "I'm just taking a peek."

Fish can be nervous in a clear-running stream without any trees in the area, so I crawled toward the brook on my knees. I was aiming for a pool below a stretch of whitewater. The ground was wet. I moved slowly, and when I made it to the edge of the stream I poked my head through the last row of weeds. Trout! There were three browns suspended in the pool. They were quietly hanging out in calm water, waiting patiently for the next hatch.

Without warning, I was struck by an unbending desire to hold the little jewels that hovered there, fins switching back and forth. "I could catch them," I thought to myself. I ran back to the truck and explained to Lynn, "This might be a good place to relax, have a snack, pick some flowers, read a page or two, make another cup of coffee and—by the way—maybe I could fish in the stream for a minute?"

"Oh, brother."

"I know."

I suppose her response was understandable, given the previous night's contemplation of fly-fishing ethics, but I couldn't help myself. I caught and released four browns before we got back on the road, and even though Lynn rolled her eyes off and on while I fished, I don't think she really minded that much. Fortunately, she finds entertainment in my obsession with fly rods, creeks, and trout.

I'll be honest though. The foul-hooked brookie I took from Rock Creek was a sharp reminder that our streams get more pressure than they should. For an increasingly large group of us, fly-fishing is the tie that binds us to our environment. But the tie is an illusion. As much as we like to think we're part of nature, the world has a way of reminding us that we are cultural and economic creatures in the end. And at the moment, our culture and our economy are on a collision course with the overall health of the nation's freshwater streams.

In *Just Before Dark*, Jim Harrison wrote, "If you are keen on trout fishing, I advise that you log thousands of hours a summer, because the signs point to its demise." Jim Harrison is wise. I think he's right, and despite my own reservations, I think the suggestion to log thousands of hours a summer is sound advice.

Jonathon Livingston Brook Trout

I once lived in northern Wisconsin on a farm two miles from a stream called the Tomorrow River. Of all the bodies of water in the Upper Midwest, the Tomorrow was my favorite place to fly-fish for trout. It's a modest creek, bobbing quietly across the landscape. It wanders through swamps where the soil is wet and black. It passes through fields where cows watch you cast, and in a few of my favorite places it saunters through forests that smell like conifer dreams.

The water in the Tomorrow is cold. It's born in a place where crystal liquid bubbles from the ground in a series of artesian springs, but at its source the river is surrounded by a treacherous bog. To fish the headwaters, you hike up and down the hills of a hardwood forest, and then you have to cross the swamp, but if you're willing to do that, you find yourself alone on a clear creek lined by cattails and hemmed in on both sides by scattered stately old spruce trees.

Brook trout are the only fish that swim the headwaters, and if you fish for brookies you don't guess about where to find them. They live in societies with norms. They follow rules when it comes to the places they call home: eddies behind rocks, shade beneath trees, the bottoms of deep pools and pockets where hawks and eagles can't reach. All of these are likely places for brookies to lay up and wait for their meals. Like many of us, they love to eat. But they like to eat without spending energy. Find a spot in a stream where fish can eat well without working hard, and you will find satisfied brook trout.

Over time, I came to know each inch of the Tomorrow, and I also met most of its fish. I'd start at the edge of the swamp where the trail meets the water, and I'd move slowly upstream, dropping flies on each seam of current, under tree limbs, and behind all the big stones. I usually timed my trips so I could fish for two hours, and then I'd hike back to the car and drive home, but I made an exception on a Sunday in April. I packed a lunch and set out with the intent to forge up farther than before.

It began as an ordinary trip. I caught four of my old friends, tiny but colorful brookies, in places where I'd come to expect them. The river was clean and the red-winged blackbirds were singing. The cattails rustled in a light breeze and the spruce trees stood guard over all of us. It was a fine day by any measure.

When I made it to the point that marked new ground I paused. I inched around the bend so I could see what came next, and it was good. A thick ribbon of water rippled over loose rock, and on both sides of the creek there were undercut banks sure to hold brook trout.

I flung my line and dropped a Pale Morning Dun close to shore. The fly fell onto the river and began gliding with the current. It was a perfect drift. The Dun moved like a bug cast down from heaven above. A fish swimming nearby watched the fly land on the water, and six feet below the spot where it came to rest the trout snatched the bug from the surface. He swam for the bottom in the beginning, and then the brookie ran upstream, but I held the line and he grew weary in the current. Still, a jump and a series of tugs ensued before I brought him to hand and plucked my fly out of his mouth. Then I eased him gingerly under the surface, and he faded back into the river.

The battle was quick, but the commotion ruined my chance to catch another trout in the same spot so I turned upstream. At the top of the run, water poured in between two boulders and the hefty stones put a bottleneck in the creek. The rocks created a stretch where the water rolled through fast and smooth. My impression was that the current was too strong. I thought, "Brookies wouldn't struggle to hold themselves in there. It goes against their values." But before I could finish the notion a fish flew out of the water and into the air over the stream. He was covered with the colors common to native brook trout: red dots circled by faint blue rings parsed out like constellations. He was small, but the fish was a sight. I stood in admiration. Then my jaw dropped when he bounced off the rock to his right while flicking his tail, adding grace and a bit of style to the move. For an encore, he dove into the river without a splash. I had to pause. I had to laugh.

I thought, "Let's see what the dainty acrobat thinks of this," and dropped a fly on the calm water over the rocks. The fly fell onto the pool behind the boulders, and then it caught the current and began drifting downstream. From that point on it was clear that I had discovered the lair of Jonathon Livingston.

The bug brought a rise out of Jonathon, just as I planned. He jumped straight up in the air a foot in front of the fly and five inches off to the side. Then he fell back down tail-first in what could only be described as a purposeful, joyous little belly flop. It was as if he meant to say, "Yes! That's a fly. It's a beauty! I'm not going to eat it, but watch me do this!"

I threw the Pale Morning Dun onto the same spot ten more times, and the fly prompted a response every other cast. There were more belly flops, arching lunges, dolphin-style leaps, and airborne lay-ups off the rocks both left and right. He refused everything I offered, but as far as he was concerned the bugs were excuses to jump and dive. As I watched him something became obvious. In the case of Jonathon, swimming was more than a way to travel or exercise. The act of swimming turned the fish into a magnifying glass, collecting light thrown off the fringes at the core of what it means to be alive.

I realized I wasn't going to catch him after my fourth or fifth attempt, but it wasn't the desire to catch the trout that kept me casting past the point where I knew he wouldn't bite. I was having as much fun as he was. I looked forward to each leap. I wanted to see what he'd try and how it would turn out. After an hour, I sat on the bank and took off my hat. I stared into the water and wondered if there wasn't a lesson in the antics of the brave fish that had just carried out one swimming exploit after another, all the while defying the conventions of brook trout society. I started walking home thinking, "Maybe it wouldn't hurt if I tried to be like Jonathon."

His wisdom sank in at the end of the week. That's when *I* started to swim. I hadn't been to a pool in years. I remembered my childhood swimming lessons, but they were unpleasant. Adults made sure the atmosphere matched that of a boot camp. "Don't do that." "Listen." "This is not the time to visit." It's no wonder I hung up my trunks at an early age. But it seemed to me that no living creature enjoyed anything as much as Jonathon enjoyed swimming, so as a grown-up I went back to the pool with his spirit as my guide. I bought a swimming suit at a local sporting goods store and found my way to the open-swim session at the YMCA.

I must say, my first time back in the water did not work out. I started having flashbacks. Everywhere I looked there were adults hollering at children. I couldn't stand to listen so I cut my swim short, but I checked the pool schedule on my way out the door and learned of a lap swimming program on the weekend. Lap swimming was different. I had a whole lane to myself. I splashed around and made waves. I kicked my feet and paddled with my hands. I worked my way back and forth enough to wear myself out and went home feeling utterly satisfied.

I rode my bike to a thrift store thirteen blocks from home and bought a silk-lined red-and-gray-plaid smoking jacket. In the years since, despite my wife's pleas to wear something less Hugh Hefner on occasions that called for normal or even formal clothes, I wore the jacket. I still do.

I love music, and that day on the river started me wondering, "What kind of music would brook trout listen to? Which instrument would they play, if they could play instruments?" I didn't have to think too long. The answer came quickly: the ukulele. I ran a search for a uke on eBay and found one for the price of a cheese calzone. It was delivered four days later, along with a fistful of sheet music and a how-to guide for idiots. Now, when I finish swimming in the afternoon I saunter home in the jacket, settle into a seat on our back porch, and jam on my ukulele. Sometimes I play through the sunset into the evening, uke songs backlit by the twinkling of stars.

The Happy Whale

Bear Tollefson and Graham Baise were my childhood friends. Bear was a typical kid, the son of a teacher and a nurse. Graham was different, however. His parents are both artists. Graham's mom is a musician and his dad is a photographer and part-time diesel mechanic.

Graham is eccentric. When we were young and overly concerned with our appearance, he cut his own hair with a pair of dull paper scissors. When senior photographs were due, he snapped a Polaroid of himself at arm's length and politely handed it to the high school yearbook editor. During the twelve years it took us to get through school, I never saw him eat anything other than two dinner rolls, a milkshake, and a fruit roll-up at lunch in the cafeteria.

I believe I would have the support of the American Psychological Association with the diagnosis that Graham's mother Susan was the source of his peculiarity. Our hometown is the living archetype of Garrison Keillor's Lake Wobegon. Tomahawk, Minnesota, consists primarily of bankers, preachers, grocers, teachers, homemakers, and Scandinavian farmers. In the middle of a population striving hard to look proper in the eyes of the lord, Susan was a smoking and drinking bass player in a late-night rock 'n' roll band.

She spent her productive time scraping a living out of rural bars and wedding dances. It put ten years on her face that don't belong there, but her life has been a grindstone, sharpening her vision. Susan sees through the baloney that most of us accept as the American way. She shunned the trappings of the middle class, so you could say that she and Graham both suffered for her art, but they lived on their own terms. Music was what mattered—more than cars or clothes or trophy homes. Their lives were like the songs they loved. By the time he turned eighteen, Graham maintained a collection of LPs that stood up like a stack of cordwood. He found himself in vinyl record albums.

As of late, American kids have been handed the task of finding themselves. In the past, women's roles were prescribed and men followed in the footsteps of their fathers. Today, without much aid from adults, young people have to figure out who they are and where they fit, all while they're still teenagers. I had to do it. I tried on roles: potter, philosopher, stock broker, doctor. I was trying to figure out who I was and what I was supposed to become. Bear and most members of my generation did the same thing.

Graham was searching too, although he was searching for something else. While the rest of us were trying to discover who we were and where we fit, Graham was patiently hunting for a mythical fish he called the Happy Whale. In contrast to the preprofessional musings of people like Bear and me, Graham was concerned with finding and catching the Happy Whale.

When Graham's parents were together they bought a home on Rainy Lake southwest of Tomahawk. After the divorce, Susan struggled to hang on to the property, but the bank won the battle. She lost the house in the eighties after Graham graduated from high school. Still, Susan's feverishly underpaid work made it possible for Graham to grow up on a lake, a proud Midwestern tradition.

In the spring, as soon as the water warmed up, Graham fished for the Happy Whale. When winter came, he sat on a five-gallon bucket in the middle of the ice, angling for a cold and hungry Happy Whale. In the fall he continued his quest alone after school, but in the summertime he fished with Bear and me.

When the three of us fished there were typically questions about where to go and what to catch:

"Perch on Gurney Lake?"

"Northern pike in Francis Creek?"

"Smallmouth bass in the Bad Medicine River?"

We always came to a consensus, but the decision didn't mean much to Graham. Wherever we ended up, he went in pursuit of the Happy Whale. It didn't matter if we were supposed to be after panfish in a pond or pike in the lily pads along the shore of a lake. Graham always chose the largest Daredevil spoon in his tackle box, and he pitched it as far as he could out into whichever body of water we happened to be on. He didn't catch a thing, as you might expect, but the act of chasing fish meant something different to him.

Graham is six months older than Bear and me. Therefore, he was the first to earn the right to drive a car. When the day arrived his dad bought him a 1974 Chevy Impala, and we were no longer bound to the tallgrass prairies and oak forests of home. We couldn't exactly quit school and light out for Jackson Hole, but we lived within a day's drive of a region almost as dramatic as western Wyoming—the shore of Lake Superior, north of Duluth. Graham's driver's license arrived in the mail, mid-July, 1985. We had the Impala packed and rolling north before the calendar flipped to August.

We'd been "up north" before with our families. We knew the lakes and rivers in the northeast corner of the state were different than those in central or southern Minnesota. In Sherburne County where we're from, rivers are the color of tea that's been steeped for a week. The water is opaque. Fish, rocks, sticks, and snapping turtles are all hidden below the surface, but by contrast, the water in the north country is clear. Once we made it past Duluth, we could see down to the black rocks on the bottoms of rivers and creeks. We even saw trout occasionally; on a footbridge over the Cascade River, we watched a school of steelhead cut a path upstream.

On our way north, we hiked past roaring rapids and we climbed the sheer cliff walls that line rivers like the Baptism, the Manitou, and the Temperance. We camped below Gooseberry Falls, drove to the town of Grand Marais, ate pizza at Sven and Ole's restaurant, and sat on the shore of Lake Superior, skipping stones until the sun went down. We were enjoying the kind of freedom that can only be appreciated by teens on their first trip away from home.

The week slipped by too fast, so we decided to take our time driving back. We headed south on Highway 51, which hugs the shore of the lake from Duluth to the Canadian border. Along the way, the route is intersected by countless creeks, canyons, and waterfalls. Thus, we agreed to stop at the noteworthy places.

Seven miles south of Grand Marais I saw a sign that said COBBLESTONE CREEK, so I asked Graham to stop. The Impala skidded on the gravel by the side of the road, and when it came to a halt we piled out and charged down the bank on the edge of the highway. We found the creek at the bottom of a deep ravine. It was little more than a trickle, but the streambed was obviously wide enough to hold more water. We were confused, because even though most of the rivers were running low by midsummer, Cobblestone Creek was too low.

We started upstream. Bear and I were both built for speed back then. We were three-sport athletes: cross-country in the fall, ice hockey in the winter, golf in the spring, and a combination of the three throughout the summer. Graham wasn't into sports, but that didn't matter. We couldn't keep up. There were settings where Graham was prone to exert himself—ball fields and ice rinks weren't among them—but rock-strewn creeks always seemed to set him on fire.

We scampered upstream for fifteen minutes. Then something unfamiliar forced us to stop. A cold gray wall of concrete stood in our path. Today I'd recognize the structure as a diversion dam, but at the time I didn't have the words to describe what I saw. Still, a brief examination made it clear. Somebody was stealing the creek.

"How could it be?" I asked.

"Who would do that?" Graham added, and Bear wondered, "Where does the water go?"

It was the first time I remember being disturbed by the sight of a dam. I've seen rivers altered nine-ways-from-Sunday in the time since, but this was the first point where I had to wonder about the ambitions that drive our decisions about land and water use. We meandered back to the car at a much slower pace. I hiked ahead of Bear by fifty feet, and Graham dropped so far behind he fell out of sight.

I stopped onshore with a hundred yards left to the car, because I wanted to give my friends a chance to catch up. I sat down beside one of the deepest pools left on the creek and took off my shoes with the intent to soak my feet in the water. But when my toes broke the surface, a silver missile emerged from the bottom. A fish with metal mirrors for scales wriggled in the shallows, then zipped back down and vanished into the depths.

I whispered, "Steelhead." Then I shouted, "Bear!"

"What?"

"A fish!"

Bear ambled up to the edge of the pool, doubtful.

"It's down there," I insisted.

He said, "I don't see it."

I grabbed a stick from the forest and poked it into the creek. Once again, the chrome torpedo raced to the surface. The fish struggled in the shallow water at the top of the pool, but he was trapped, and when he finally resigned himself to that, he swam back down to the bottom and disappeared again. Bear and I were left staring into the darkness.

He said, "I don't believe it."

"What did I tell you?"

"I think he's stranded."

"Yeah, he's trapped."

"Let's go get Graham."

We sprang back up the creek toward Graham, whom we found hiking slowly, shoulders sloped. I said, "Graham," with the most earnest face I could pull together, "it's the Happy Whale. We found the Happy Whale, and he's trapped downstream."

The three of us rushed to the edge of the pool and I did the same trick with the stick. The fish made another frantic but futile attempt to escape, and we sat with our eyes bulging out as the trout made a series of desperate runs back and forth.

Graham asked, "How did he get stuck way up here?"

"That doesn't matter," I replied. "It's the Happy Whale."

"You're right. It's him, and he's trapped. We have to do something."

Bear said, "I agree. We have to take him back down to the lake."

We scratched our heads. We didn't have a net, and we

didn't have a fishing rod either. The Happy Whale probably wouldn't have taken a lure anyhow. I said, "We don't have anything but the clothes on our backs," and my point sparked Graham's imagination. He was grinning at Bear with the kind of smile you'd expect to see on an inmate when he finds the key to his cage. Graham reached over and tugged on Bear's T-shirt and said, "You're wearing a net. Take it off; we can use it. We can catch the fish in your shirt and then carry him down to the lake."

Bear didn't buy it. "What about the sleeves? He'll wiggle right out through the sleeves."

"We'll tie them up," I suggested. "We'll tie a knot in each sleeve. We'll make a big, wet bag out of your shirt. We'll catch him and carry him down to the lake like Graham said."

Bear was outvoted. He took off the shirt and we tied up the sleeves. We even found a way to knot the neck shut. By the time we were through we had a 100 percent cotton, Fruit of the Loom purse net.

I was the first one into the brook. It was my job to corral the fish toward the top of the pool, and Bear waited there with the T-shirt. I went in over my knees to start. It was cold. I was shivering, but I had a responsibility. I started moving toward the center of the creek where the Happy Whale was hiding, and our plan began to work. Once the fish figured out I was in the water he made a dash for the top of the pool.

Bear was there with the shirt, but the fish slipped around him by a foot or maybe two. The next thing I knew I was up to my waist, inching toward the hiding place at the bottom. The fish had nowhere to go, and what commenced was a little unruly. I was cold, the fish was scared, Bear was dubious about the plan, and Graham was on the bank shouting, "There he is, catch him!" I can't say how it happened, but after a brief bout of splashing around, Bear came up with an eight-pound steelhead writhing in his T-shirt.

We ran downstream toward the lake because we knew the fish was tired. The water in the pool was probably warmer than he would have liked, and if the energy he spent trying to avoid Bear's T-shirt wasn't all he had, it was close.

We kept him in the wet shirt on the way back down to the road. Bear and I ran over the highway, gunning for Superior, and Graham stopped at the car to get his camera. The fish was alive when we made it to the shore, but he was gasping.

Bear stepped into the lake and eased the fish down in the water. He held the Happy Whale by his tail and tried to revive him by pushing and pulling him back and forth. The strategy helped. The Happy Whale was coming to life, and Graham was onshore enlisting the photographic service of a tourist.

He asked a man in a loud floral shirt, "Can you take our picture?"

The man said, "Sure," and Bear hoisted the fish out of the lake.

Graham stood on one side and I stood on the other, proud as parents at a graduation. The stranger snapped the shutter, a flash went off, and Bear set the squirming fish back down into Lake Superior. The Happy Whale swam slowly in the beginning, but he eventually picked up speed. We strained our eyes to follow him as he faded in and out. Then he disappeared beneath the waves.

It's not every day a Happy Whale swims into your life. It's even more uncommon to be called upon to save one. I suppose we're all searching for a Happy Whale in some way, and you never know when or if you're going to find one. Today, I'm not sure I'd know a Happy Whale if I held one in my hands, so in light of my age-inspired ignorance, I play it safe. I set all of the fish I catch back below the surface carefully. I think of Graham, Bear, and the sound our voices made when we used to laugh until we were exhausted. Then I grin and return to hurling my line out over the empty water.

Working-class Glass

By the time I tried fly-fishing for the first time it was the early 1990s, and by that point the fly rod had been through three transformations. Since the 1800s, fly rods had been built with split canes of bamboo. Then in the 1970s we began to fashion them from spun glass fibers. But glass fell out of favor ten years later, and our staffs of fiberglass were replaced by graphite sticks. Until recently, with the exception of a bamboo rod I received as a Christmas gift, graphite was all I knew, and I didn't question it too much. I was comfortable with the status quo. That is, until eight years ago.

I was struck by a notion in the spring of 1997. As part of the process of courting my would-be wife, it occurred to me that I ought to buy my lady friend, Lynn, a fly rod. We were living in northern Wisconsin, surrounded by cold water and brook trout. I was spending more than my share of time chasing fish, and I figured if my plans for a wedding were going to work out, I'd better involve Lynn.

The shopping ritual began, as it often does, at a high-end fly-fishing specialty shop in an upscale part of town. I was happy to drool over their elegant rods and reels, but the prices were out of my range so I drove to a popular sporting goods warehouse. I saw some possibilities in the stadium/store, but the atmosphere wasn't great. I'm big on ambience, and the retail arena didn't feel right.

That left me with one option. Like most towns in the Midwest, our city was home to a lonely bait and tackle shop set in an unseemly neighborhood where weathered paint, sagging roofs, and broken windows were the norm. I drove past the store each day on my way to work. I thought, "Why not?"

Cobwebs were the main feature of the interior design, and to complement the webs there were aluminum landing nets hanging from the walls. In the middle of the shop there were piles of crank baits, pork rinds, and spinning lures stacked on slouching sheet-metal shelves. A row of live wells shaped like laundry tubs lined one side of the room, and a quick stroll past the tubs revealed a plethora of animals: leeches, shiners, crawdads, and a few things I didn't recognize, all of them waiting for the day when they'd be impaled and then flung over one of the neighboring lakes.

Behind the counter sat a man who struck me as an identical twin to the person in the "This is What You'll Look Like if You Smoke Cigarettes" poster, the one the American Lung Association used to scare children in the 1970s. His hair was disheveled and oily; his face was lined with creases you couldn't put in your pants if you tried; there were bags under his eyes like kangaroo pouches; and his lips were permanently pursed to accept the ubiquitous cancer stick. Less than an arm's length away, there sat a black plastic ashtray buried under a mound of sickly orange butts.

"How goes it?" he bellowed.

"Not bad," I returned, thinking, "I'm going to make this fast."

"What can I do you for?"

"I'm looking for a fly rod. A gift. Something for my lady friend."

"Fly rod?" he puzzled. "No fly rods. Used to carry 'em. I don't know what happened. Folks stopped askin' for 'em, I guess."

While he thought about his customers' buying habits, I perused the only rack of rods in the shop. It was a tight mess of dust-covered spinning gear: Ugly Stiks, Abu Garcias, and foam-handled Berkeley Avengers. But to our mutual surprise, at the far end of it all, there stood a marigold-yellow fly rod. It was a six-foot, five-weight, Eagle Claw "Sweetheart," complete with a little red heart-shaped symbol stamped near the hook-keeper.

I plucked the rod from the rack and gave it the old retail waggle. It was the first time I'd ever laid hands on a fiberglass fly rod. It was more flexible than the graphite I was used to. I was intrigued, but the rod wasn't for me, and I knew the details of its construction weren't going to matter anyhow. I knew a technical explanation of rod materials and their qualities wouldn't inspire Lynn, but I had a feeling the heart-shaped symbol might pique her interest. Three minutes and twenty-four dollars later, I was headed for the door with the Sweetheart under my arm.

It wasn't graphite. It wasn't the latest or the best. It wasn't a bamboo classic or a classic of any kind. Even so, I had a hunch the yellow rod would make Lynn happy, and at home my intuition was confirmed. She loved it. At this point she didn't know much about fly rods, but that didn't make any difference. The gesture was not about fishing or tackle. This was a way to create common ground. The little yellow stick was a perfect excuse for us to spend time together in the woods.

I bought the Sweetheart early in the spring. That meant we had the whole summer to ply the waters of Wisconsin. We fished the Wolf River, the Prairie, the Plover, and the Peshtigo. We fished lakes by canoe, and we fished a few ice-cold spring ponds reminiscent of the glaciers that once covered the area. We caught fish everywhere we went, but mostly we reveled in the warmth and freedom of long summer days spent with brook trout in our midst.

I'll be honest, though. The warmth and freedom were more important to Lynn than the brookies. By the end of the season, after a few token casts, she'd slip back onshore to look for brightly colored rocks or the perfect pinecone. Lynn didn't take to fishing like I thought she might, but we were together, we were outside, and that was really the whole point. Besides, since she wasn't that excited about angling, I knew she wouldn't mind if I borrowed the Sweetheart when I fished the Tortoise Shell River.

The Tortoise Shell is a classic Midwestern stream. Its headwaters lie in the tamarack swamps and muskeg bogs of the north woods, and its lower stretches run through rolling hills pocked by dairy farms and hardy fields of corn, barley, and wheat.

Like neighboring Minnesota and Michigan, Wisconsin was once covered by white pine and hemlock trees so tall and thick toward the top that they formed a canopy over the land. The canopy shielded the ground from sunlight, and the arrangement created a parklike setting where a person could amble through ancient forests unobstructed by brush.

The lumber barons oversaw the wholesale removal of those trees in the 1800s. Thankfully, the forests have returned. But they're not the same. They're thick. In some places they're downright impenetrable, and they cover the hills and valleys beside many of my favorite streams, including the Tortoise Shell, where the forest envelops the river in a tube of tangled branches and leaves. It is no place for a nine-foot fly rod.

With Lynn's permission, I started packing the Sweetheart on trips to the Tortoise Shell. It was the rod's diminutive length that appealed to me at first, but it was the feel that made me wish the Sweetheart were longer and more useful on lakes or in wide-open spaces. It was the bend and sway, the graceful manner of the glass, that made me wish all my rods had the same laid-back disposition.

I grew fond of the little Sweetheart, but there were limits to the affair. It was too short for all but the most tree-snarled creeks. In addition, it was marigold yellow from tip to reel seat, and it was embossed with a heart-shaped symbol. I wasn't about to jump out of my truck, open the topper, and expose the Sweetheart in front of my macho fishing friends. I would have been the laughingstock of Langlade County. So there I was, falling in love with fiberglass, but it was a clandestine affair limited to solo trips on wood-choked streams where I cast the glass in secrecy.

We left the Midwest before I had a chance to look for an eight- or nine-foot fiberglass rod without the girly moniker. In the summer of 2001, Lynn and I sold our furniture, rented a trailer for our books and clothes, and struck out for Casper, Wyoming. I had accepted a post on the faculty at Casper College.

We were excited about the move for a number of reasons, but Wyoming is a long way from Wisconsin, in more than just miles. There would be no more quiet casts to brook trout poised in soft rippling streams or calm spring ponds. I realized that if I was going to fish in my new setting, I was going to fish big, strapping rivers—the North Platte in particular.

Wyoming is home to a wide range of waters, but in Casper, the North Platte River is the only game in town. It's a good game. If you had to choose one body of water to have close to home, it might be the Platte. There are tailwater sections close to town, and the river supports healthy populations of both browns and rainbows, some of whom are giants. Unfortunately, there was nothing in my arsenal of three- and four-weight brook trout rods that would help me catch fish in Casper. I didn't have the right equipment, and I was unfamiliar with the technique of fishing weighted flies underwater, a method called "nymphing," which is a standard practice on rivers in the West.

Luckily, the historian Thomas Renn took me under his wing early in my first season. For Tom, fishing is a form of scholarship. He approaches the selection of flies and the rigging of rods the same way he approaches source documents penned in the seventeenth century. He brings the keen eye and mindset of a well-trained academic to the process. Since I tend to approach fly-fishing the same way I approach a Sunday game of Frisbee in the park, we're perfect partners. He brings all the knowledge and equipment that we need to catch fish, and I bring beer. On our first outing I brought a six-pack of amber bock and the strongest rod I owned—an eight-foot, four-weight.

When we found our spot beside the river, we started gearing up. Tom handed me a strike indicator and two split-shot sinkers. I thought, "Sinkers and bobbers?" I asked myself, "Can this be right?"

Along with the sinkers and a strike indicator, Tom gave me some good advice about mending line and managing a drag-free drift, but I didn't listen. I was so baffled by the prospect of hurling the lead-and-foam menagerie back and forth with my four-weight noodle rod that I couldn't think of anything other than my equipment and the unlikelihood of catching a fish with the outfit. Truth be told, I didn't catch a single fish. I watched Tom land three brawling rainbows, and I was happy to give him a hand with the net, but I was clearly not on board. I needed a stronger fly rod, and I also needed to read and think about fishing with nymphs so I could understand what I was trying to accomplish out there on the Platte.

The reading came first. A trip to the county library turned up an early edition of Ed Engle's *Fly Fishing the Tailwaters*, and also a copy of *Fly Fishing the North Platte River* by Rod Walinchus. Both are excellent. With time, I came to understand the feeding patterns of our local salmonids, and at some point I finally accepted the proverb passed down by old-timers at fly shops in the area, "On the Platte, the trout don't ever look up." I bought a plastic dispenser full of split-shot sinkers, and I started leaving my dry flies at home.

With respect to a rod, I garnered advice from everyone I could think of who had ever caught a fish on the North Platte River, and the counsel was consistent. The consensus was that I needed a nine-foot, six- or seven-weight rod, with brands and models ranging all the way from moderately priced graphite, to not-on-a-teacher's-salary, not-if-you-want-to-stay-married. I took the suggestions of all the fly-fishers I knew, but even as I listened to veteran casters extol the virtues of graphite technology, I kept harking back to my days on the Tortoise Shell, Sweetheart in hand. In the end I was determined—it had to be glass.

Without further contemplation, I called Clark Davis of Pleasant Prairie, Wisconsin. Clark is regionally famous for his collection of vintage bamboo rods, but I knew from his Web site that he held on to a handful of old fiberglass rods as well. In fact, at the time we talked, he had a nine-foot, six-weight rod he was willing to part with. "Perfect," I thought to myself. It was a custom job—black fiberglass blank, half-wells grip, and gold-wrapped guides. He didn't know the rod builder, and he wasn't sure which company rolled the blank, but I like a little mystery, and the price was right, so I bought it.

Roughly one month after my first fly-fishing trip in Wyoming, the rod I call "Black Bart" arrived at my doorstep. It was a Tuesday, and by Wednesday afternoon Tom and I found a few hours to fish the Platte. As usual, I watched him fight and land three of Casper's finest.

I was anxious to catch my first rainbow on the river, so I studied Tom's technique. The uncanny thing about his approach, the thing that took the longest time for me to understand, was the curt and concise nature of his casts. Tom drifts his flies three feet in front of where he stands. Through the eyes of a brook trout fisherman, the strategy borders on the absurd. For years I'd been making long casts to mistrustful little brookies who were frightened by any sign of motion on the stream. But North Platte rainbows don't mind if you steal their turf. They don't even mind if you stand beside them in the current. The water's heavy green tint blurs their vision, and given the raw number of fly-fishers on the river, fish accept anglers as features of their environment. I began reciting a mantra: "There are no brook trout in the North Platte."

Over the course of the afternoon, I practiced the skills I

watched Tom use successfully, but at the end of the day I was fishless, and I was feeling low. The sun started setting and I stopped thinking about trout. The color of the sage-covered hills at dusk lulled me into a prairie-river daze, and it was from this trancelike state that I watched my strike indicator slip below the surface at the end of a long, slow drift. It took a moment for the strike to register, but when it did my instincts flew to my forearms and I pulled up on Black Bart.

I was bound to a leaping, plunging, hard-running Platte River rainbow. The rod bucked and heaved as the fish used its length as a lever in the current. The glass gave enough to keep my tippet from breaking, but the rod's backbone was strong. The fish eventually tired, and after a five-minute battle I brought the proud silver pugilist to the net—my first fish on the North Platte—courtesy of a modest old fiberglass rod made by somebody I'll never know and purchased for less than the cost of a meal at a Chinese restaurant.

I understand old fiberglass rods aren't for everyone. Their charm is subtle. It takes a mischievous streak to appreciate their qualities. For instance, if you occasionally call your rod a "pole" in front of your highbrow fishing friends just to watch them squirm, you're a candidate for glass. If you drive a Lincoln Navigator but you wish you still owned the Volkswagen bus you sold because "it wasn't practical," you could easily aspire to a vintage fiberglass rod.

Let's face it, old glass rods are the Volkswagen vans of the fly-fishing world. They're not Ferraris or Land Rovers.

They're not fast or responsive, but in upscale cars and trucks, the vehicle is the focus of the drive. You pay more attention to the car than you pay to the world outside. In a Volkswagen van, it is the scenery that matters. Likewise, with a fiberglass rod in hand, it's about the water, the fish, your friends, and the sun sinking under the horizon, casting memorable shadows on the day.

For what it's worth, in this era of uptight, high-priced, nose-in-the-air angling gear, I'm going to keep carrying honest, understated fiberglass rods to the river. It's the best way I have found to soothe my trout-and-cold-clean-river-loving soul.

Carp Unlimited

July ninth is Parade Day in Casper, Wyoming. The town shuts down. Businesses close, streets are blocked off, and we let small children out of summer school. It's a party all the way from 9:00 AM until noon, but I always wonder what to do afterward. This year, I gave my wife Lynn a look that said, "What next?" and she reminded me why I married her by asking, "Why don't you go fishing?"

The parade put a dent in my day so I couldn't stray far from the house, although I don't have to travel far to go fishing. The obvious place to try was Gray Reef Dam on the North Platte. It's a blue-ribbon trout stream twenty-five miles from home. On that note, I've been advised not to brag about local fishing holes, but I don't mind boasting about the river that runs through Casper. It's not a secret. Half the population of Colorado can be found on the Platte any day of the year, and Parade Day was no exception.

When I made it to the dam I found it crawling with fly-fishers, so I kept driving. I discovered the next public access point was crowded too, but there were no cars at the following spot, a parking lot next to a stretch called Gambler's Run. I thought, "It's a fair distance from the best water but still worth a try." I was wound up, so it took no time to rig my rod.

I grabbed my waders out of the truck, stuck a foot in one leg, and then realized it was too hot for rubber overalls. When it's warm I get to fish in swimming trunks and wading boots, my favorite angling costume. With a trusty six-weight rod in hand, I slipped my scantily clothed self into the cool water of the North Platte.

I should mention that the nature of the Platte is such that you end up bobber fishing, even with a fly rod. Fly-fishers call their bobbers "strike indicators" in order to distinguish themselves from their bait-casting cousins. But I say, "Call it what you want, a bobber is a bobber." In truth, whether you call your strike indicator a bobber or not, it's understood that dry flies don't work on the Platte. They're fun to cast, but they don't catch fish because the water is full of food. There's a smorgasbord of bugs hatching off the bottom all year. Trout have no reason to dine at the surface where they're preyed upon by eagles.

Since the river is flush with insects, the trout grow to ample size, but there is also a downside to the fertile nature of the stream. The water is green. It's so green you can't see the trout you're after and they can't see you either. The trick is to get a weighted lure—a Pheasant Tail nymph or a San Juan worm—down deep where the fish like to feed. But you're groping in the dark. It's a puzzle. You cast into areas that look like houses for trout and you hope they're home and hungry.

I fished the first run without any luck, but before I had time to change methods my attention was drawn upstream. I caught sight of an unmanned rowboat drifting down the river. It looked like a white dinghy bobbing with the waves, nobody onboard. I watched the boat roll with the current, but before I could switch my verdict the vessel opened a pair of wings and lifted itself up off the water. White pelican. They're huge. At a distance it's easy to mistake them for rowboats. On land I once mistook a pelican for a Toyota. I'm not a birdwatcher, but I can see how people become members of the binocular-toting set. It's an inspiration to watch a bird like a pelican fly.

The birding was good, but I hadn't caught anything yet so I decided to move downstream. I didn't want to waste a chance to catch a fish on the way, however, so I lobbed my fly into the waves and strolled down shore at a pace that matched the speed of the water. My strategy worked. A rainbow hit the San Juan worm I was walking like a dog on a leash. He shot into the air, arched his spine, and crashed back down into the current.

His runs were forceful. He strained against the pressure of the line. He shook his head, dug with his shoulders, and slashed his tail, but despite his effort I brought the chrome torpedo in toward the bank. I don't measure fish, but in this case my twenty-four-inch net wasn't long enough. The only way to nab the trout was to bring him in bent. He was bright and healthy. I held him for a moment. Then I watched him fade back into the river.

One trout of that size is normally all I need and I'm satisfied. A catch like that and I usually find a spot onshore to lie down and think about the contours of the world, but I got a late start. The parade ate half my day so I kept fishing. After an hour, I noticed two real drift boats coming downstream, so I moved to the side as a gesture of courtesy. I knew the boatmen would stick to the center because it was the only place where the river was deep enough to keep them afloat.

After stepping aside I stopped watching. I focused on the stretch in front of me, but I happened to look over my shoulder in time to see the guides hop out and drop anchor on a sandbar. I had company: four men and two women. The women didn't look like they belonged on the river, and since it's widely known that I'm not sexist, my reputation as an open-minded man shouldn't be tarnished if I mention it was obvious the ladies spent more time fixing makeup than they did selecting flies, rigging rods, or reading water. Furthermore, I noticed that two of the four men wore caps bearing the emblems of Colorado teams: the Broncos and the Avalanche. They were "greenies."

Allow me to explain. The people of Wyoming are resentful toward their neighbors on the south side of the state line, and when our bitterness bubbles to the surface it is displayed in a tendency toward name-calling. Here in Wyoming we call people from Colorado "greenies." I am not proud to say that I bow to the tradition, but I do. I've been indoctrinated.

When Lynn and I moved to Casper we found a house we could rent to own. We were newlyweds, and we figured real estate would seal the deal. But this was our first home, and we didn't know anything about houses, so we decided to have the place professionally inspected. I called around and discovered that local home inspectors were too busy or expensive. I was ready to give up, and then I found Will Harris. We didn't talk long on the phone, but I could tell by the sound of his voice he was an old-timer, an expert.

Two days later Harris knocked on the door and I was confused. I expected a white-haired geezer in overalls. Will Harris is thirty-five. He's an old man trapped in a young man's body. I know a few of those. In fact, Lynn describes me that way when she's with me in a mall and I'm shopping for a cardigan or a pair of Hush Puppies.

Harris moved to Casper from Kentucky at the age of twenty. In the 1980s, he didn't care about careers. He came for the fish and game. He fell into a job in construction and from there he became a home inspector—a good one. I followed him around the house because I wanted to learn what I could. I was his shadow all morning. I walked behind him blurting questions about roofs, furnaces, and electricity. The nature of the questions didn't make a difference, however. He answered my queries with the zeal of a contestant on a TV game show.

Near the end of the inspection Will asked, "Do you like antelope?" and he added, "as table fare?"

I said, "I don't know. I've never eaten antelope."

He said, "If you need it, I have a recipe for pronghorn that'll change your life," and he went on, "What about trout? Do you fish?"

I grinned and said, "Yeah. I fish a little."

When he was through we sat at the dining room table. He began his report, and I started writing a check. While we were both scribbling he asked, "Do you have an atlas of Wyoming?" I said, "Yeah. One second."

I laid the atlas on the table and opened it to the page marking the region west of Casper. He pointed to three of his favorite fishing holes and then put his pencil on a popular part of the North Platte River. He said, "You have to fish this hole on a weekday. On the weekend there'll be greenies everywhere. If you try it on a Monday or Tuesday you should have it to yourself." Since I had asked close to a hundred questions already, I didn't ask what a greenie was, but I was curious.

The only time I ever heard the word "greenie" was in middle school. When a member of my sixth-grade class refused to blow his nose we called the drip that formed a "greenie." My mind whirled as I tried to align my understanding of the term with the question of what I would find if I fished this stretch of the North Platte. I didn't ask. I shook my head as if to say, "Yeah. Those greenies."

I took my question to work the next day. I asked a colleague, "Hey Jim, what's a greenie?" Jim is well-known as a wise man. He said, "We call people from Colorado 'greenies' because they drive cars with green license plates."

That sounded logical. In fact, the explanation made so much sense I thought that was all I needed to know, but I was wrong. In the moment after I posed the question Jim's brow shrunk into an angry set of ridges, and I could feel his temperature rise. He went on to say, "They crowd our streams because two-thirds of their rivers are toxic and the ones they haven't ruined yet are lined with McMansions sporting KEEP OUT signs on trees in the yard and I don't know what they're reclusive about since pretty soon they're not going to have anything left to keep people out of there are so many newly planted pilgrims on the Front Range of the Rockies watering lawns with the runoff from these God-blessed mountains it's all going to dry up and blow back East anyhow do you know what I'm saying Hanson?" I managed a brief "Uh-huh," but this was new to me. I grew up in Minnesota, and we told Iowa jokes, but they were mild. We had to make up phony stories about Iowans because we didn't really resent them.

And there I stood, elbow-to-elbow with six greenies. I know I'm not alone here. Every fly-fisher I know values the sport at least in part for the solitude. I was a little put out, but I didn't let them spoil my day. I kept casting and smiled when we made eye contact. It was a pleasure to simply enjoy the after-noon. Then they caught a trout. I thought, "OK. Sharing my run is enough. I am not about to let them out-fish me too." I couldn't take it. I reeled in, slogged back to the truck, and took off in a cloud of billowing dust.

I drove to a place called Lawson's Bluff, two miles east of Gambler's Run. The bluff lies at the end of a gravel road that leads to a stretch of the Platte where public access is allowed. It's a popular place to put in and take out drift boats. People rarely wade the bluff, although I am not sure why that's true.

The area is picturesque. The river rounds a sweeping bend near the boat launch, gray cliff walls line the left bank, there is a channel near the bank known to hold large trout, and there's a slough that follows the river alongside the road. The slough is full of algae and carp.

"Carp?"

I like rainbow trout. I really do. But by this time I was finished drifting weighted flies through the depths of the river with the hope of catching fish that might not even be home. Carp tend to swim in shallow water. You can see carp, and you can hear them too. They're big and they thrash around in the weed beds close to shore. "I'm going carping," I thought to myself.

The last time I drove by the slough I sat on the bank for an hour watching carp swim around like submarines on maneuvers, but this time there was a herd of cattle in the backwater. In fact, there were cows everywhere. I couldn't get the truck through the herd, so I pulled off the road and onto the shoulder. Then I stepped out and discovered the cattle had made a mess of the area. It was nothing but mud and dung where I stood, so I started downstream. I strolled the bank until I reached a point where there was still water in the slough, and I found a school of carp. The cows were keeping them from enjoying part of their former home, but the fish were holding to the last stretch of water in the swamp.

I hustled back to the pickup, honked my horn like a lunatic, and pressed through the herd. Once I made it past the cattle, I parked the truck and sat on the tailgate thinking of flies. I caught carp when I was a kid, but I used worms or dough balls. Since I didn't have either of those I chose a Vanilla Bugger instead. I thought, "What fish could resist something as savory as this?"

With my choice of fly set, I walked back to the water's edge. I dropped the Vanilla Bugger three feet in front of a fish headed upstream, but he didn't notice. I cast the Bugger toward a carp wrestling a make-believe enemy in the weeds, but vanilla must not have been his flavor. I couldn't coax him either.

Meanwhile, a shiny new truck pulled up behind me, pushing its license plate out in front like a green badge of courage. No doubt the driver was curious about the fisherman who had eschewed the North Platte for the slough. He held back at first, studying the fish and my technique. Then he eased alongside and asked, "Dude, are those brown trout?" My mischievous streak stood up as if called to attention. I produced a baffled look and said, "Would I be flinging flies at them if they were bottom-feeders?"

"No. I suppose not. Those trout are huge!"

I whispered, "Welcome to Wyoming."

Then he said, "I have to get my buddies," and he was gone.

As I walked along I saw four carp moving upstream in a wing formation so I laid my fly on the water over the front-running fish. The lead carp didn't look twice. As he swam past the fly sank to the bottom, so I jiggled it a bit, just in time for the next carp in line, but he was frightened and he peeled off to the right. The third fish was unaware of my efforts, so I started reeling in and the motion caught the attention of the last carp in the squad. He chomped the fly in a swift, bobbing gulp. I set the hook on time, my line came off the water, and I was tied to an aquatic dinosaur with knowing eyes and golden scales.

The carp steamed away like a cruise ship bound for port. He made a run upstream, scattering his peers. Then he changed direction, and on his way back he caught sight of me standing onshore, which set him in motion again. He made another turn, my reel spun like a wheel, and my backing began to unfurl. The carp made lightning runs up and down the slough and all I could do was watch my line cut the surface of the water back and forth until his fins tired out.

When the fish grew weary, he started swimming in circles in front of me and I faced a dilemma. I'd been standing onshore because the water was rank and the bottom was too soft to wade. But a thick row of weeds lined the bank, and I couldn't get the carp close enough to unhook him. I had no way to reach the fish, not unless I hoisted him out of the water, and my line was too light for that. I knew if I tried to lift the carp I'd break my tippet. I had two choices. I could cut the leader and set the fish free with a fly in his lip, or I could go in after him and dislodge the hook properly. I started leaning toward the strategy of snipping the line, and then I saw into one of his eyes and I couldn't do it. Bottom-feeder or not, this was an honest fish and he put up an honest fight.

I stepped into the murky stew and sank to my knees. Then I trudged through what amounted to generations of wet cow dung, edging toward the fish. When I reached him I hefted him by the belly, plucked my hook from the corner of his mouth, and set him back down in the slough. That was all the carp I ever hoped for. I walked over to the main branch of the river and washed the filth off of my legs.

On my way back to the truck I started thinking. I caught a brawny trout in the early part of the afternoon and a missile of a carp before the day was through. Which was more challenging? Good question. Which fought harder? It is tough to say. Which has a permanent file in the office cabinet of my memory? The bottom-feeder.

I was still thinking of the carp as I drove away from the bluff. I had to pause when I reached the last intersection before I turned toward home, because the fellow in the pickup was rounding the corner. He had two buddies with him. I could see them in the windshield—eyes akimbo, hearts pounding, minds full with the thought of sight-fishing to monstrous trout. I couldn't keep a smile from widening my face. I drove off the gravel onto the highway and made a pledge, "I'm mailing a check to the local chapter of Carp Unlimited."

Apache Trout

My childhood was intertwined with Bear Tollefson's. We played hockey on the same team in the winter, ran cross-country in the fall, golfed when the weather was warm enough in Minnesota, and fished for walleyes at his family's summer home on Lake O'Grady. Bear's father was a fisherman. He was a schoolteacher by trade, a pipe-smoker, and also a tier and caster of flies. The Tollefsons spent most of the summer at the lake, plumbing the depths for walleyed pike, but for three weeks out of each year, walleyes did not suffice. In August Bear's dad drove the family west for the sake of tossing flies at fish called "trout" on rivers like the Gibbon, the Firehole, and the Yellowstone.

Most Midwesterners know little of trout or mountain streams. Apart from a glimpse at a stringer of brookies in Montana at the age of twelve, I hadn't seen many trout myself, but Bear's stories of the land out West enlightened scores of children. We listened as he told tales about elk, buffalo, white pelicans, and fish caught with tiny hooks hiding in tufts of feathers.

We parted ways after high school. Bear moved to Minneapolis to attend the University of Minnesota, and I left for Mankato State. Mankato is known as a place for kids to sow

their oats, and in my first year at "State" I did my part. I tried
to see how far oats could be sewn. As a freshman I whirled
through a frenzy of introductory classes, part-time jobs, and
parties where beer bongs were as common as coeds. On a
memorable morning in March I woke up on my neighbor's
kitchen floor, staggered across the small apartment, caught
a look at myself in a mirror, and said to no one in particular,
"Maybe it's time to move out West."

I toured the southern Rockies in a Volkswagen bus over
spring break. At the apex of my journey I passed through
Flagstaff, Arizona, and I was stunned. This was the place I kept
buffed and polished in my imagination. It felt like the region
in Bear's stories—dry air, high elevation, ponderosa pines and
mountainous peaks. When school let out at the end of May I
packed my things, drove to Flagstaff, and stayed. I transferred
from Mankato State to Northern Arizona.

In year two of my education I laid plans to spend the
summer in Prescott, a small town at the base of the Bradshaw
Range. I had a job lined up providing care for a child with
muscular dystrophy. I bought a map of the Prescott National
Forest, highlighted the creeks and hiking trails, and mailed it
off to Bear. I knew he was going to graduate, and it turned out
he was ready for the West. We decided to meet.

Bear drove down to Flagstaff, and when I finished school
we set out for Prescott together. I started work the day we hit
town, and by the end of the week he found a job at a local
organic food co-op. In the beginning, we rummaged through

forests outside the city, looking for a place to camp for the summer, but we discovered that water was hard to find. There were a number of brooks in the area, but they were seasonal and the biggest were tiny by our standards. Still, we found a stream that suited us. It was a section of Carson Creek winding through a canyon of stone. The walls and streambed were cut of one piece, and they shined because they'd been scoured for centuries.

We left our vehicles on the topside of the canyon in a stand of pines, and from there we used a game trail to pack our gear down to the bottom. We left our camp stove and beer cooler on a rock, and when our parents asked, "Where are you living now?" we both delighted in answering, "We live on a stone sticking out into Carson Creek." Our stint on Carson lasted more than a week, but we were restless so we searched for other sites—deeper canyons, wider streams.

At one point we fell in with a band of college kids. From them we learned about Arizona's Mogollon Rim, a transitional zone that runs east-to-west through the center of the state, dividing it in half. The north side of the rim is a long high altitude ridge, but the elevation drops quickly. The land is ushered down to the state's central deserts in a series of staggered cliffs and peaks. The area is a geological staircase bounded by the city of Sedona to the west, New Mexico on the east.

The high country on the rim is handsome, but its most striking features are the brooks and streams that wind their way from the forests on top to the desert below. Over too many beers and a makeshift meal of tortillas and cheese, we learned of a creek that wriggles and bobs through a canyon that cuts down through the rim—Cloud Creek—a wet jungle in the dry heat of the desert.

We made our first trip to Cloud Creek in June. Our acquaintances warned us not to go in my VW. They explained that we'd need four-wheel drive to reach the trailhead at the base of Cloud Creek Canyon, so we took Bear's pickup truck. Twenty miles from the stream our jaws unhinged. Towering buttes and purple mesas filled the distance. Cacti stood as tall as trees, coyotes scuttled through the brush beside the truck, and quail fluttered from their hiding places as we rolled past their homes on the high chaparral.

We parked after we found the trailhead. According to our directions, we had a half-mile hike to the stream. We set out with confidence and stumbled onto the creek after a walk down a trail winding through a grove of ancient cottonwood trees. Eventually, the path opened onto a place I can only describe as the world's finest swimming hole. We stepped over a rise and looked down on a turquoise pool lined by broken orange rock. At the top of the pool, the stream poured in between two boulders the size of freight cars, and the over-sized stones pinched the creek into a long, swift chute. Years before, I'd been to a spot on Oak Creek called Slide Rock State Park, and the arrangement reminded me of places where tourists slid along on their butts. I told Bear about Slide Rock, and I started pointing out how the chute on Cloud Creek might work the same, but I didn't get to finish.

Bear is a renegade. He'll try anything. Before I could give him instructions on how to posture one's self while riding a surge of current, he dropped into the chute and disappeared. I caught a glimpse of his arm midway through, a foot and one of his sandals bobbed at the surface, and then he vanished again. Finally, he popped up from the center of the pool wearing a wide, impulsive grin. It was our personal water park.

The chute was fun, but it tired me out, so I decided to rest under the branches of a willow on the bank. Meanwhile, Bear climbed up on a rock and stared into the water. We found paradise. I fell asleep, and when I awoke I caught sight of something I'd seen before. Bear was on point. Like a well-bred German shorthair his head angled down toward the creek, his back was stiff, and he stood stone-still. You see, most of us wear the heavy and restrictive coat of Civilization wherever we go, but in the case of Bear Tollefson the coat is a windbreaker, tossed aside the moment he leaves the concrete-and-drywall world we call Society. On a remote river, Bear's senses match those of any creature in the wild.

In a loud whisper I asked, "What is it?"

"Fish," he shot back.

"What kind?"

"Not sure."

"Are they big?"

"No. They're small, but they're pretty."

"Are they trout?"

"Get up here!"

There were two kinds of fish in the pool. At the bottom were pikeminnows, but in the shadows, no doubt alarmed by our presence, there were trout. At the time I didn't know a rainbow from a brown. A trout was a trout. They were all pretty. That's as much as I knew, but Bear had been out West each year since he was three. Even he was puzzled. He said, "I'm not sure what they are." Then he asked, "What kind of trout do you have around here?"

"I don't know."

"They look like rainbows."

I stared at the pale forms swimming in place at the edge of the pool. Then I remembered an article about a rare and elusive tribe of trout: the Apache.

"They're Apaches," I declared.

"Apaches?"

"Yeah. They're endangered. Eastern Arizona is the only place left where they can be found." I said, "We are in Apache country, my friend."

"I don't know," he mused, "they look like rainbows."

We went back the following week. We went in with full packs and plenty of food because we planned to stay for three nights. On our hike upstream we stopped to make a run through the chute. We splashed in the water. Then we climbed out into the parched desert air and draped ourselves over sun-warmed boulders to dry. It *was* paradise; a dreamworld tucked inside a gorge of sandstone stretching a thousand feet from the streambed up toward the sky.

When we were dry we started hiking again. Two miles in, we reached a point where the stream ran out of a narrow slot in the canyon with sheer cliff walls on both sides. We couldn't find a path around the gorge. The only way to continue was to wade, but the water was too deep. We would have had to swim, and we weren't prepared for that. We hadn't packed our things in plastic and we couldn't afford to soak our clothes, food, or sleeping bags, so we made camp. We unpacked our gear and pondered our plight over a pouch of convenience-store jerky.

The canyon made a turn midway through, so we couldn't see the other side. We weren't sure how far we'd have to swim to reach the end, but by dusk our curiosity was too much. We dove in. A hundred yards later the walls opened up and we came to rest in shallow water, but we were tired and the sun was setting. We didn't waste time. We caught our breath, swam back to camp, and slept like two downed trees.

I was the first one to wake in the morning. I stumbled over to Bear's spot on our rock, nudged his shoulder with a stick, and whispered, "Bear. There's a scorpion on your chest." His weary eyes flickered open and his drowsy morning face burst into fright. Instinctively, he swatted the creature from inside his sleeping bag, and the jolt sent the little beast high in the air. When it landed the scorpion scampered off to the side.

"Good morning," I said.

"Yeah. Right."

The day that followed can barely be described. I've never

felt so much like Huckleberry Finn or someone along those lines. Upstream we found more slot canyons and deep green pools to cross. In one case, we used an old cottonwood as a ferry. We saddled up on the trunk, kicked with our feet, and paddled with our hands. We moved slowly, necks craned skyward, eyes fixed on untold layers of sandstone laid down in stripes over periods of time neither one of us could imagine. In our excitement we forgot about trout. I did, at least. Bear did not forget. He was scouting for fish the whole time. He was still convinced the trout in the creek were rainbows, but we couldn't see them well enough to say for sure.

On our way back to camp I asked Bear about fly-fishing. He mentioned that his fly rod and vest were in the truck, but he reminded me that we'd each need a license if we were going to fish, and he added, "For those we're going to need money." We didn't have any money. On paydays we filled Bear's truck with gas and bought food for a week. Then we'd take a stroll down Prescott's Whiskey Row and we didn't leave there with anything but pocket change. Fishing was out for financial reasons, but I could see Bear's brain gears turning. He said, "I have an idea."

"What is it?"

"Diving mask."

"Diving mask?"

"Yeah. I have a diving mask in the truck."

"You do? Why?"

"I don't know. But I have a diving mask. I'm snorkeling

all the way up Cloud Creek. If there are Apaches there, we'll find them."

We went back at the end of the week. Bear brought his diving mask and I carried a pair of goggles I found at a grocery store in Prescott. We also brought four dry bags borrowed from a bouncer at a bar, and one of Bear's coworkers loaned us a pair of boogie boards, the kind they surf on in the ocean. Everyone was happy to lend us equipment. Of course, we explained that our outings were scientific, humanitarian, conservationist endeavors. We described how we were in pursuit of Apache trout, and we assured our benefactors there was reason to believe the remaining members of the tribe were hiding out in the brooks of the Mogollon Rim.

We packed our food and clothes in dry bags, stuffed the bags into packs, lashed the packs to our boogie boards, and swam the gear bundles across all the deep pools and sheer-walled canyons of Cloud Creek. This time, with our eyes protected by glass, we swam with the fish in plain sight. Bear was right, the trout were rainbows.

That didn't make any difference. I still clung to my hope of finding Apaches. Cloud Creek became home. We camped outside of Prescott when our work duties called, but eventually Bear would ask, "Do things seem cloudy to you?" My response was, "Yeah. I don't know why, but everything seems cloudy." Then we'd buy enough food for a week and set out for Cloud Creek Canyon.

I don't know if we actually saw an Apache that summer,

but we gave it everything we had. We swam and dove like a couple of porpoises up and down the stream—through rapids and riffles, underneath waterfalls, and across emerald pools at the bottom of steep-walled chasms. Just to be complete, we paid a visit to Pine Marten Brook, a similar creek four miles to the east. Bear doubts it to this day, but I think I saw a school of five Apaches on that trip. I guess it's something for the Game and Fish Department to decide. I hope I was right. I hope for all our sake there are still Apaches left in Arizona.

Wyoming Native

I read an essay by John Gierach called "Kazan River Grayling" in the summer of 1998. At the time I'd never seen an arctic grayling. I'd never been to Siberia or the Yukon Territory, and I missed the grayling in Michigan's Upper Peninsula by three-quarters of a century. There were healthy populations in the UP until 1925, but at that point, natural historians agree, an unknowing angler plucked the last grayling from an Upper Michigan stream. That fact saddened me for years. I lived in northern Wisconsin during the 1990s, and I spent many summer days and nights in the UP fly-fishing for brook trout and smallmouth bass. It pained me to know that grayling could have been, but weren't on the list of fish I caught and released.

Lynn and I moved to Casper after the turn of the century, and when I bought my first fishing license in the Cowboy State I walked out of the tackle shop with a fistful of maps and pamphlets. The Game and Fish Department gave me plenty to pore over on cold winter nights when I couldn't be out on the water. In the brochures, I discovered that grayling weren't native to Wyoming, but I also noticed there were lakes in remote alpine regions of the state alleged to support a small number of survivors held over from stocking efforts in the 1970s. Of all the areas that looked agreeable to denizens of the arctic, Reed Lake seemed like the most likely place to find grayling.

Reed Lake is set up high in the Cloud Peak Wilderness near the top of the Bighorn Mountains. It's only accessible on foot or by horseback; I don't have a horse, but I figured I could hike to Reed Lake in an afternoon. I would camp for two nights, fish for three days, and then hike out to the truck and drive home.

There was a point in my life when my highest ambition was to pack into the wilderness as far and as often as I could. That was a long time ago, but I still have enough gear to make the process possible. I aired out my sleeping bag, dusted off my tent, cleaned my camp stove, and stuffed it all in my pack. Then I pitched the pack into the back of my truck and set forth out of Casper, headed toward the Bighorn Mountain Range, pulled along by the vision of a high mountain lake and the possibility of grayling.

The parking lot at the trailhead was full, but I reckoned, "It's a big wilderness. I'll find solitude." I put the pack on my back, readjusted the hip belt to accommodate my waist, and started hoofing up the trail toward Reed Lake. The path was steep. I discovered that even though my camping gear had aged with dignity, my muscles hadn't. I ached. Two hours in, my heels were raw meat, and my back was beginning to resist the prospect of carrying the pack another mile. Finally, I came to a crest overlooking a freshly melted glacier: Stone Lake. With my feet and spine opposed to further hiking, my mind proclaimed, "Stone Lake—this looks like a good place to stop for the night." The lake was only three miles from the truck, but it put me in a position where I could take two day-hikes to Reed Lake without my pack, wearing the sandals I brought in case my boots disagreed with my feet.

My blisters and back, painful as they were, changed the nature of the trip. All of a sudden I had an afternoon to myself that I didn't plan to have originally. I decided to go fishing.

Stone Lake was the first body of water on my route, and it also marks the intersection of four different hiking trails. Backpackers headed in any one of four directions all pass by Stone Lake on their travels. I fished there for half an hour, but I didn't catch a thing. Stone Lake sees more than its share of anglers each summer, and I guessed I was probably too late to have any luck, so I picked trail number seventy-nine for a stroll; it looked like a good place to prospect for fishing holes. The trail winds away from the lake, and then it meanders up over a ridge before it plunges down into the verdant Oscar Valley. The Oscar is a long, deep basin. It is home to a sizeable bog and a small brook called Moose Creek.

On my descent into the Oscar, I heard the familiar sound of water washing over the rocks of a riverbed. After a short hike I caught a glimpse of the stream, and eventually the trail crossed the brook on a bridge made of old logs bundled up by rangers. The creek is a narrow torrent under the hiking path. It runs fast and white, losing altitude in a hurry. I stepped off the trail and hiked downstream to see if I could find a fishing hole but there were none, so I sulked back to the bridge, disappointed.

From the bridge I tried to forge a route upstream, but it was like plowing through a briar patch. Nonetheless, I stuck to it, and after a while the brush on the bank spread out and grew sparse. The valley turned into a peaceful marsh, the kind where you expect to see moose standing knee-deep in swamp grass, snacking on leaves.

Moose Creek is pocket water. It meanders along in the pool—riffle—pool—riffle—pool progression that fly-fishers love so well. I started hiking upstream onshore, and at every turn the water grew deeper and more amenable to trout. I found hiding places and feeding troughs around each bend.

I sat down on a stump and tied on a fly. I was too tired for a study of aquatic insect life, so I crossed my fingers and hoped I could lob any old fly into the ordinary places where trout lie and they'd bite. I was right. After three dubious casts and a brief encounter with a tree branch, I lofted an Irresistible Wulff onto the water above two brook trout laying in wait. When the fly touched down, the larger of the two sprang to life. The brookie slurped my bug off the surface and then dove with the fly in his mouth. My rod tip bounced like a ball as he searched for a place to hide at the bottom, but I played him quickly. I brought the fish to hand and removed my hook from the corner of his jaw, but I held him for a moment before I turned him loose. Every spot of red and every circle of blue reminded me of brooks and trout I'd known in the past.

In the Midwest, I fished for brookies exclusively. They're native to Wisconsin, and they are the most abundant trout in the northern half of the state. But it occurred to me that Wyoming was well outside their native range. Pretty as they were, I wondered what the little devils were doing here. There was only one possible answer, of course. Somewhere along the line, somebody decided that brook trout were nice and they stocked Moose Creek with fingerlings. I could tell the stream was now home to a healthy population, but I didn't mind. I thought, "So much the better for me," and prepared to cast again.

There were brookies in all the pools. They were hiding in the riffles, too. I found them hunkered down behind logs, and they were holding to the shore below Moose Creek's undercut banks. I caught four more as I worked upstream. They were small fish, but the largest of them was twelve inches long—enough to bend my three-weight noodle rod right down into the reel seat.

As the afternoon came to a close, the sun started setting, and I decided to head back to camp. On a small stream, it's hard to fish places you've already contaminated with your presence, but enough time had passed since I'd been through, I thought I'd give it a try. I walked back to a point just upstream from a spot where I expected to find fish, and I floated my fly toward a deep bow in the creek.

At the cusp of the bend, the fake bug disappeared. It was sucked underwater by a trout. I raised my rod and the pole buckled. This was the largest fish of the day. He was heavier than the others I'd caught on Moose Creek, but when I had him in close I could tell that he wasn't a brook trout. My eyes strained and my mind reeled. I wondered, "What do I have here?" After the fish grew tired I brought him to hand and it was clear—cutthroat—my first since I moved to Wyoming two years before.

I studied my colorful catch. Those nights spent pouring over pamphlets paid off. I recognized the trout as a cutthroat of the Yellowstone variety. His sides were tan. Tan! After years spent stalking silver, yellow, pink, and green fish, here I stood holding one that was wonderfully, beautifully, unmistakably beige. A loose set of black spots covered his back, and the red stripe on his throat beamed. I turned the fish loose and he rushed back to deep water and safety.

I stayed right where I was, thinking, "Cutthroats are the only trout native to the central Rockies, but I just spent a whole day catching brookies that by all rights belong back East." For that matter, I was standing at the end of an entire season spent catching fish that don't have an historic or biological place in the region: brookies, browns, and rainbows.

It was obvious to me as I held the fish that a cutthroat trout is a reflection of the Wyoming landscape. The cutt's khaki skin was a complement to the dry, sage-colored carpet that covers two-thirds of the state. The cutthroat was part of this place in a way that brook trout never could be.

It occurred to me as I stood knee-deep in Moose Creek

that each species of trout has evolved in such a way that they mirror their native places. The blue-black sides and bright red spots on brookies are reflections of dark, humid forests speckled with wildflowers blooming in the lush native home of the little char we call a trout. Likewise, the bold spots and golden tone of German browns echo the ecology of the European chalk streams that were once their sole residence, and there is no better symbol of the cloud-enshrouded Northwest than the rainbow.

I walked back to my camp in a fog of reverie. I drank a cup of tea, nestled down in my tent, nodded off to sleep, and dreamed of Charles Darwin, the Galapagos, and the nature of species.

I took the hike to Reed Lake in the morning. Without my pack, the trip went well. The trail ended on a ridge overlooking the lake, although a steep wall of boulders stood between the end of the path and the shore. I began the descent cautiously, but twenty yards from the water I watched a grayling leap from the lake to gulp a bug, and with the fish in sight I lost my sense of self-preservation. I finished the descent fast and reckless.

On the bank, I rigged my rod in record time. I threw a cast, my fly fell on the water, and a burst of chrome crashed the surface—my first arctic grayling. He weighed less than a pound, but his lengthy dorsal fin gave him extra stature, and the silver scales on his sides produced a varicolored sheen, like oil on a parking lot.

I set him down in the water and tossed my fly again. Same thing—smacked by a grayling. On my third cast, I caught number three. On cast number five I reeled in another. I was starting to see how the grayling's appetite could have led to its demise. They took everything I threw at them. They weren't big, but they were aggressive, which meant they were easy targets in the Midwest. Anglers simply took too many from Michigan's lakes and streams. Now here I was, catching and releasing grayling in one of their last strongholds in the lower forty-eight. It felt good to reel them in and set them free.

But, I have to say, the cutthroat from the previous day changed my mind about non-native species. The indigenous fish cast a long shadow over the arctic interlopers on Reed Lake. After I'd seen a native fish up close, grayling seemed to lose their luster. I wondered what possessed the stewards of the state's fish and game to make such a radical change in fish-stocking policy. I wondered what drove them to move so swiftly toward welcoming non-native species to Wyoming.

I thought about the first year *I* spent in Wyoming. Personally, I wasn't welcomed too warmly. I applied for a position at Casper College in 2001, and I gladly accepted the job because I'd spent some time in Wyoming, and I knew the state would suit Lynn and me; we both believe a town's elevation should be higher than its population, and the Cowboy State is home to many such places. We moved to Wyoming in August and by September we had completed a three-goal hat trick: we were married, bought a house, and "settled down." Fly-fishing was the only thing left to do.

With a new driver's license in my pocket and a song of joy in my heart, I waltzed into the local sporting goods store, laid my cards on the counter, and requested a trout-fishing license. The clerk 'spent a moment scanning my identification and declared, "Nonresident. Seventy-five bucks."

I chuckled, "That must be a mistake." I said, "Look at the address. I reside up here on Thirteenth."

He claimed, "You're a nonresident until you've lived here for a year."

I couldn't believe it. In the coolest, most patient voice I could muster, I said, "Listen . . . friend . . . I'm employed by the state of Wyoming. I own a piece of Wyoming. The piece of Wyoming I own is just up the street. That's my address. It's my house. I live there. Can you look me in the eye and tell me I don't 'reside' in this state?" He could. He did.

I was flabbergasted. I didn't buy a nonresident license. I didn't go fishing either. I went home and whined to Lynn, but she wasn't faring any better as a Wyoming rookie. She's a hairdresser, a damned good one, but the board of cosmetology wouldn't accept her credentials. She sent the necessary forms to the appropriate offices in Cheyenne, but the papers always came back without an official stamp of approval. She made phone calls to all of the people who could possibly help, but it didn't make a difference. Some days I'd come home and find her in tears. For months it looked like she wouldn't be able to work in our new home state. After a yearlong struggle, she finally talked to a helpful secretary on the phone, and she was granted the right to practice her trade. But it didn't come easy.

Thinking back on the process of becoming Wyoming residents, I concluded that if the state exercised as much discretion with fish as they did with my wife and me, we'd have a lot more cutthroat and far fewer non-native species.

It was my final day in the Bighorns, and I had a decision to make. I thought about hiking back to Reed Lake, but my memory of the native cutthroat on Moose Creek was gnawing at me, so without too much deliberation I packed a sandwich and an apple, slipped back into sandals, and bid farewell to my campsite one last time. I traipsed up trail number seventy-nine on a return trip to the Oscar Valley. But my luck was different on day three. I fished four previously productive pools without a bite. At first, I thought I might have made too much noise, so I stalked upstream along the bank. I crouched down and slipped quietly beside the water's edge, but that didn't help. I still didn't catch any fish. Then I looked up and noticed somebody was watching.

There was a man in his early twenties walking downstream toward me onshore. I gave a nod, and he tipped his baseball cap. When we were close enough, I could see that he carried a spinning rod in one hand, and in the other hand he carried a stringer of dead and dying trout—two dozen at least. That's twenty-three more than you're allowed to keep on Moose Creek.

Plus, it might have been my imagination, but it looked like the biggest fish in the lineup was the cutthroat that had captured my spirit just two days before.

The hair on the back of my neck started twitching, my shoulders drew tight, and my chest puffed out for what seemed like a probable row. I imagined myself as the main character in the 1970s film *Billy Jack*. I was overcome with ire and a lust for retribution. I wanted to avenge those trout the same way Billy Jack avenged his people when they were wronged. I felt compelled to whack the kid upside his head with the stringer of fish.

Just then, another fellow approached from the same direction. This one was jolly enough, but he was clearly a partner to the first trout poacher I saw. He also carried a spinning rod in one hand, and in the other he was holding a Styrofoam cup, no doubt full of worms. Not even the cleverest trout can resist live bait.

All of a sudden, I realized my technique was not the source of my bad luck. I'd been beaten to the creek by two trout-poaching bait casters—and a can of worms. I was incensed. My mind raced through all the possible things I could say to the two of them before I became a whirling ball of fists and feet. At first, I thought I might try the obvious, "It looks like you killed a few trout here this morning." But I also considered sarcasm, "I see you guys don't exactly practice . . . catch and release," and I gave some thought to asking a pointed question, "Are you two familiar with the concept of a bag limit?"

Ultimately, I didn't say anything. Eventually I cooled down, and after a while I even started thinking I could find their camp and show them how to cast flies and turn fish loose. I thought about letting them try it. I began to think this might be a good chance to teach two young fishermen a lesson about the tenuous nature of trout populations. I thought this might be an opportunity to educate two, probably unwitting, poachers.

I fished a while longer and then walked back to the bridge where the trail crossed the creek. It didn't take long to find the men I was looking for. They were camped ten yards from the water, but when I approached them I could see they were in the presence of an older man, probably their father, or maybe an uncle. He was kneeling on the ground between their tents cleaning trout on a breadboard, and there were entrails scattered all over the ground. Their camp was a real fish-gut extravaganza.

They were in a state of intense concentration, so they didn't see or hear me, but frankly I stayed quiet and kept my distance. I knew, come nightfall, they were going to get a lesson, although I wasn't going to teach it. Their camp was about to become a zoo. It was obvious to me that when the sun fell the area would be busy with black bears, crowded with coyotes, and raided by raccoons—all enchanted by the prospect of finding and eating discarded fish parts. Justice was in the process of being served, so I turned and walked back to my tent.

I hiked back to the truck and drove home to Casper in the morning. Without even stopping at the house, I parked downtown in front of the army/navy surplus store. I'd never been inside before, but I walked in like a regular and bought a bumper sticker that says "WYOMING NATIVE." Who will know?

Seeds of Westerly Migration

After college, my dad took a job as a first-grade teacher. As of 1974, he'd been at the head of a classroom for five years. It is possible that first graders are God's chosen people, but they're best enjoyed in moderation. After half a decade, Dad started to think about his options and he found an opportunity in Browning, Montana. Browning Elementary needed a principal. Dad sent a letter, and two weeks later the school board invited my parents out West for an interview.

We were Minnesotans at the time, and our ties to prairie lakes and hardwood forests defined us as people. Our identities were forged in accord with the ruffed grouse and white-tailed deer that shared our address in the Upper Midwest. We were modest folks, inhabiting a humble landscape not known for inspiring leaps of spirit, but rather, quiet reflection. Montana was a foreign country as far as I knew, and it must have seemed like a faraway land to my mother and the rest of the family too. For that reason, Dad started calling the trip to Browning a "vacation." The term took the edge off the prospect of moving.

In June, my parents packed my kid sister Jess and me into a two-toned AMC Pacer, and we started down the freeway that crosses the plains. As we pushed our way through seemingly endless fields and pastures, I noticed the resourcefulness of

South Dakota's citizens. What the state lacks in natural features it's made up in cultural oddities. As I recall the trip across the wide, flat belly of America, the sights and sounds of industrial tourism echo through my memory: Wall Drug, the Corn Palace, and Reptile Gardens. At one point, we watched a curiously confident man wrestle a crocodile before a cheering crowd. Eastern Montana was a similarly treeless but welcome alternative to the roadside quirks of the interstate in South Dakota.

This was our first trip to the West. It was the first time I ever saw sage-covered prairie. It was the first time I had to squint against the white western sun, and it was the earliest point where I remember filling my lungs with the bone-dry air found out to the left of the corn belt. We didn't dawdle after we said goodbye to Reptile Gardens. We drove straight to Browning, but the parched hills of Montana left impressions.

Dad didn't tell my mother that Browning was on a reservation. In anticipation of the trip, I remember paging through brochures peppered with pictures of Glacier National Park, but I don't recall any photographs of Browning. The images etched in my mind as we rolled into town lie firmly in place, however. The pictures include "Still Life with Appliances in the Yard" and "Portrait of a Blackfoot Indian with Twenty-six Rusted Jalopies." The poverty of the reservation opened my eyes. A good student, I read western history in school, but that doesn't prepare you for the human train wreck that is the result of a century's worth of broken treaties, bungled policies, and ill-begotten work by a crooked Bureau of Indian Affairs. The Blackfeet reservation was more than a long way from Minnesota. Economically, it could have been another planet, and even though Dad was up to the challenge, Browning, Montana, wasn't my mother's kind of town.

The interview went well so we spent the next day looking at real estate. I could see the optimism on Dad's face as we hunted for a house, but Mom's response to every one of the hovels we toured was no. No. No. We left town before lunch, and we never went back.

In the spirit of vacation, Glacier Park was next on our list of spots to visit. We spent the afternoon ogling bison on the shoulders of highways, but we eventually made it to a campground inside Glacier. Once in the park, we found a campsite on a rise above a stream called Boulder Creek. You could hear the water from our site, but by the time we finished our dinner of corned-beef hash and crackers, the sun had set and dusk had turned to dark. Jess and I had to wait until morning before we could investigate.

After breakfast, we scampered through brush and down a hill to find the creek that provided music to accompany our dreams. We'd come from the land of ten thousand lakes and at least as many rivers, but none compared to this. The water might have come from the tap on a sink. By contrast, in our part of the country, rivers and creeks are the color of well-creamed tea. You can't see below the surface of our waterways, and even if you could see into our streams, you wouldn't see too much because the riverbeds are brown. Boulder Creek danced over a bed bejeweled with cobbles of red, white, yellow, black, and green. I sat on the bank with my eyes boring into the water. It was a miracle—such clarity.

As I watched the creek slide over its bed a man strolled down from a neighboring site carrying a long fishing pole. The pole's length wasn't the most unusual thing about it, however. When he started casting, the line was visible in the air, bright and thick like string.

Dad saw us watching with fascination, so he ambled over to explain. He talked about the physics of fly-fishing, said something about mass and velocity, then hiked up to the campsite and grabbed our spinning gear out of the Pacer. He came back down and said, "Look . . . we can fly-fish too . . . in a way." He opened our tackle box and pulled out what I would recognize today as a crappie jig. It was a fly! We could fly-fish! We did! All day! We didn't catch a thing! Neither did the man from the other site. Thinking back, his bad luck was linked to our commotion. We were having a ball, but we were noisy.

After lunch it was time for a nap and we all slept hard, but before the alarm was set to ring we were stirred by the sound of a group making camp in the site beside ours. Dad stepped out of the tent to greet the newcomers. I could hear their voices, but I couldn't decipher the words. Then Dad shouted, "Chad, come on." I poked my head through the canvas door and saw him pointing to a man with long brown hair and an unruly beard. The hairy man held a stringer of fish: gunmetal green with burnt orange fins, and red spots strewn on sparkling wet sides.

"Wow. What are they?" I asked.

"Brook trout," the hippie chimed, "twelve inches long . . . a pound apiece . . . best fish on Earth."

Dad agreed.

We spent the rest of the trip immersed in a pool of reverence. Western Montana was more eye-pleasing and inspirational than we could have known by reading brochures. We hiked through forests of ancient spruce and Norway pine, fed squirrels by hand in our campsites, and drove above the tree line on soaring mountain roads. Then it was over.

We changed direction, and towns started blowing past like railroad ties bucking by a train—Bigfork—Butte—Bozeman—Billings. Back home I began judging the fish in our lakes and streams by the standards of Glacier Park, and it turns out Rocky Mountain brookies are a hard act to follow. We have perch, walleyes, and bluegills in the Midwest. They're all pretty, I suppose, but something inside of me was starting to smolder. Ghostly images of brook trout were swimming in and out of my consciousness like smoke in the breeze above a campfire.

Those images linger in my memory, and I wonder what I would have become if Dad had moved us to the mountains. Would I have a different sense of self or identity? Would there be cowboy boots in the closet in place of my Birkenstocks? Would I drive a diesel pickup instead of my aging Volvo wagon?

Would I still work to protect the wilderness left in the West? Would I take it for granted? Would I be half as in love with cold, clear water and trout? I don't know the answers. All I can say is the trip to Montana planted seeds in my mind, and those seeds grew. I left home for the West at the age of nineteen, but I'm still a Minnesotan.

Black Canyon

Young men are easily obsessed—trains, cars, guitars, boats, and motorcycles. I started with canoes, and I'm currently fixated on cameras, but in the 1990s I became smitten with mountain bikes. It wasn't my fault. At the time, the city of Tucson, Arizona, engendered a zealous devotion to bikes. I'm not sure if it's still true, but in the 1990s if you set one foot in town you fell in love with bicycles.

As a student I couldn't afford the two-wheeled wonders I worshipped in magazines, so I took a job at the Spoke 'n' Wheel with the understanding that employees get discounts. The wages weren't great, but the mechanics in Tucson rode the most exotic bikes available to mortals and I was proud to count myself among them.

I met Brock Layton at the Spoke 'n' Wheel. The forces of fate brought us together, and what began there was a friendship that felt like a brotherhood. We rode our mountain bikes all over the Southwest. In the winter months we toured the ranges outside Tucson. Then when the heat came on in the summer we'd drive north to Utah where the air is cool and the hills are the color of rust.

After routine rides in the desert, our tradition was to retire to the house Brock shared with his lady friend Kelsey. Their backyard was a hundred square feet of sun-baked dirt—a good place to sit outside on plastic chairs, drinking Mexican beer out of mason jars, lime slices floating in the suds. On an especially warm night in August we sat listening to a blend of canyon wrens and Chet Baker with our feet propped up on milk-crate ottomans. At a break between songs, Brock stepped into the house and Kelsey talked to a neighbor who drifted into the yard.

When Brock came back he carried a tube, three feet long and two inches wide. He tossed it at me from the porch.

"Is this what I think it is?"

"Yeah. It's a fly rod. Open it."

The tube was well crafted. I put pressure on the cap and it moved in circles like a lock on a safe. I took the lid off the cylinder and pulled out a sheath of fabric. Over the years, I've had plenty of fishing poles, and I always did what I could to keep them from breaking, but a rod tube and a cloth bag? This was serious. I removed the cloth and unveiled a four-piece St. Croix Emperial. Brock explained that it cost three times more than I ever paid for a pole. Months later, I learned that St. Croixs are inexpensive rods, but that's because fly anglers are vulnerable. At the peak of their obsession they pay six or seven times more than they should for equipment. St. Croixs aren't the most expensive sticks in tackle shops, but they fling fly line with grace and dignity.

I assembled the rod. I slid one ferrule into the next until all eight feet of graphite swayed as one. Brock tossed me a reel and I fixed it to the seat. Then I jiggled the pole back and forth, up and down. I couldn't find words. I'd seen fly-fishing on television, but this was the first time I held a fly rod in my hands.

It was more eye-pleasing than spinning gear. Fly rods have an aesthetic quality that distinguishes them from their bait-casting brethren, but apart from its length and appearance, the rod had a different character. It was flexible. It felt like a spring. I looked at Brock and said, "It's whippy." Brock laughed and replied, "I thought so too at first, but they're made that way on purpose. You should see it cast. It's the next best thing to throwing a Frisbee. It's the spirit of Zen in motion."

Like good college-educated white liberals, we dabbled in Zen Buddhism, and even without a stream in the vicinity I could tell Brock was right. The rod had a Zen-like quality. It drew my thoughts into focus. Even in the yard it demanded all of my attention. The cacti, the neighbors, Chet Baker, and the canyon wrens—they disappeared. For several moments there was only the pulse and rhythm of the graphite staff cutting through the dry air of the desert.

Fall semester started three days later. On the first day of class I cashed in my financial aid check and drove to Tight Loops, a fly shop on the eastern edge of town. You wouldn't expect to find a high-end, full-line, fly-fishing spe-cialty store in the desert, but the shop is well established and successful. There are no trout streams in Tucson, but the dreams of streams that live in the Southwest are strong enough to support a healthy market for fly rods, vests, and long-billed caps of various kinds.

The shop is owned by Cole Ivins, angling evangelist. The moment I walked through the door I could tell he saw me as a disciple. I spent the better part of the afternoon in the store. I hadn't ever tossed a fly on a stream before, but we talked for hours about trout, rivers, and fishing strategies.

I test-drove six rods in the parking lot. Cole didn't know I was poor, and I didn't let on, so I cast fly rods that cost as much as I made in a month. Maybe it was inexperience, but the most expensive rods in the shop did not impress. To my beginner's mind, they felt like two-by-fours. They didn't bend. Cole described the rods as "fast," and he explained that "speed" was a good quality, but I was not convinced.

In the years since, I've come to agree that fast rods work well in some settings. For instance, in Wyoming you have to chug your line into gale-force winds barreling down from Canada on the plains. Fast rods are meant for these conditions. But on spring creeks, and in canyons where the only wind is your breath on the water, whippy noodle rods are best. I walked out of the shop with a St. Croix identical to Brock's, along with a nagging question about how to pay for textbooks.

Over the years, Brock and I both made trips to a stream called Branch Creek, a brook winding through a canyon in the Green Mountains of Arizona. But our explorations on the creek had been for the sake of hiking and swimming. We saw trout, and we thought about trying to catch them, but we weren't equipped to fish. Since that was no longer the case for either of us, we planned a trip to Branch Creek in October.

We decided to drive to the top of the canyon near the headwaters. The hike to the bottom was steep. It took half an hour to reach the creek, although the trip seemed shorter. The stream was always within earshot. It was loud. Onshore we had to raise our voices over the roar of the brook wrestling the rocks in its bed.

We looked for a place to camp when we reached the bottom and it didn't take long to find one. There was a site with a fire ring two paces from where we stood at trail's end. We dropped our packs and started sifting through gear. We were eager to fish so we didn't even pitch our tents. We put our rods together, dug our flies out of our packs, and rushed to the bank.

Our site was perched on the edge of a stretch of rapids. The whitewater was a pleasure to watch, but neither one of us knew how to approach it with a fly so we hiked upstream. We walked alongshore searching for a calm pool or quiet run. A hundred yards later, we reached a point where the creek poured in from around both sides of a boulder. We suspected the stream would be crowned by a quiet pool up above, and we were right. We shimmied around the stone and found a pool on the other side. Above the rock, the creek was as still as a looking glass; the water mirrored the gray and khaki canyon walls. That was enough to make us smile, but below the surface there was something odd. Through the calm water we could see the bottom and it was dark. The varicolored rocks we learned to love on hiking trips were gone. The streambed was as black as freshly dug coal.

I asked, "What happened?"

Brock said, "I don't know."

"Is it some kind of silt?"

"Let's see."

Brock stepped into the water and reached down toward the bottom. He said, "It's dirt. It's like soil, but it's thick. It covers everything."

We discussed the possibility that Branch Creek had been cursed. Brock said, "The stream looks like it's been struck by a plague or some kind of blight," but we'd come a long way. We decided that whether the stream was black or white, we had to try our flies. Then we watched a circle form on the water. A fish slurped a bug off the surface.

Before I could send a cast out toward the ripple we heard footsteps from behind. We paused for a second, and that's all it took for our company to wander into view. It was a forest ranger following up on a report that heavy rain had fouled the creek. We talked for a spell, and he explained that a farmer had put the plow to his acreage upstream. Three days of rain washed the loose soil into the water, and when the silt finally settled it painted the streambed black.

I asked for an assessment of the damage, and he explained the bottom would be black for the rest of the year, but he was confident a good spring flood would wash the silt out of the canyon. If so, he assured us, our multicolored streambed would be back.

The ranger carried a pack and a telltale fly rod tube. Brock asked, "How about the fish? Have you caught anything?" He said, "I stopped fishing an hour ago. I caught five rainbows on dry flies. They took everything I threw at them." As the ranger turned to go Brock asked, "How do you get a gig like that?" He said, "Just luck, I guess," and a pause filled the air. Then the ranger added, "No. I paid my dues," and with that he disappeared around the bend.

We didn't pay attention to the water while we talked with the ranger, but the moment he left we turned our eyes back toward the creek. There were three more rings on the surface—subtle signs the fish had been dining while we were distracted.

The canyon walls were tall and the bank was narrow where we stood, so we took turns casting. Brock went first. He shot his Blue Winged Olive out toward the last ring to form, and we watched the fly waft into the air and drop onto the creek. *Puck.* The fly was plucked off the water by a trout on the lookout for bugs. I watched Brock wrangle the bright fish-jewel to shore and then release him; a rainbow in the desert.

It was my turn. It took a while longer but the steps were the same—careful presentation—anxious moment—green shadow swimming up from below—*puck* at the surface—rainbow trout in tow. I turned the trout loose and we moved upstream. We fished nine pools through the evening. As the ranger said, the

trout were indiscriminant. I can't say whether the black streambed influenced their appetites, but the fish were hostile. Light
pucks turned into assaults. At one point a rainbow soared out of
the water a foot in front of my fly. Then he crashed in on top of
the vulnerable bug, mouth open, teeth flashing. He attacked it
from the sky. Our flies were battered by the end of the night.

We ambled back to camp in the rich light of dusk,
exhausted. We built a fire, boiled water, ate soup, and drank
tea. We talked about trout and fishing with flies. We were new
to the sport, and we were spellbound. We were also at stages
in our lives when our habits were starting to change. The
eating of pizza, the drinking of beer, and the riding of mountain bikes were the three pursuits that defined our days on
Earth up to this point. Beer and pizza are still important
to me, but questions were starting to form in my mind with
respect to bicycles. I wondered how long I'd continue to risk
my life by flying down the sides of mountains on too-thin
knobby tires.

Mountain bikes appealed to me because a high-speed
roll down a steep trail forces you to concentrate. It's a mind-
sharpening Zen-type affair. You're engaged in a whirling dance
with death, and if you allow distractions to take you out of the
moment, even a fleeting thought can wipe you off course and
down a path toward bodily harm.

The element of risk is obvious, but mountain biking provided me with a respite from the mild chaos of life. We all need
time to focus. Cycling gave me a break from the jumbled din

of work and school. But I was eager for a new technique, one that wouldn't contribute to the mounting number of scars on my body. I told Brock I could see fly-fishing as a new kind of Zen getaway, and he agreed. Fly rods and trout center you in the moment.

We took three more trips to Branch Creek in the year that followed. In the spring, high water washed the silt from the canyon, but the forces of time also uprooted Brock and me. He was whisked to the ocean. He's in the Northwest hurling caviar at steelhead, and I'm hunkered down on the short-grass plains of Wyoming. These days I've noticed we both avoid risks if we can. When we aren't fishing, we jog, swim, and cross-country ski—tame pursuits by any standard. What can I say? We survived our twenties and that used to seem unlikely.

Swimming with Trout

"Should we try upstream?"

"All right. It couldn't be worse."

It was a slow day on the North Platte for my friend Emmett and me. It's said that a drift boat guide can put you in touch with twenty-five trout in a single afternoon on the Platte, but those of us who wade don't fare as well. For us, five hookups are likely. We usually wrestle one or two fish all the way to the net. If we catch three it's a good day, and we get skunked every once in a while. Oh hell, we get skunked a lot. North Platte rainbows are finicky. They're big—enormous in fact—and that's what keeps us out there even on slow days, but Wyoming trout are more discerning than the panfish I used to pluck from ponds in Wisconsin.

We'd been fishing a promising run near Lawson's Bluff all morning long and we were both starting to smell a skunk, but days like these motivate you to try new things. Days like these push you to light out for new territory, and in this case, we decided to try an area that we'd seen before but never bothered to fish: a bend in the river half a mile from the bluff.

We started slogging upstream toward the bend. We began in the shallow water near shore, but the shallow water didn't last, so we moved up and walked along the riverbank. We strolled down a slim beach unobstructed for a quarter of a mile, but then it became obvious we would have to surmount a wall of rock if we were going to continue. I went first, and when I made it to the crest of the ridge, I looked down and found a sign posted on the ground below. I read the sign out loud. "KEEP OUT."

Em said, "What? I'm halfway up."

"No. Sorry. It's a sign. There's a KEEP OUT sign posted here."

"I was afraid of that. Take a look. There's a sign on the other side of the river too. We'll have to double back, get the truck, and drive up to the bend."

"Are you kidding? All we have to do is get back in the water. No one owns the riverbed. We'll stay in the water until we're past the private land. Then we'll hop back out and do whatever we want."

Emmett shook his head and said, "You're not in Wisconsin anymore. It doesn't work like that in Wyoming. Whoever posted these signs owns both banks and the riverbed too."

"The riverbed too," I wondered out loud. "How could that be?"

This was my first encounter with western water law, and as it turns out, the laws governing public waterways in the West are different than those you find in the Midwest or the East.

After Em convinced me that I couldn't just trudge up the river, we turned and headed back to the truck, but I wasn't happy. I ambled along explaining that rivers are public entities in Wisconsin. I said, "They are part of the Public Trust, like the air we breathe," and I added, "no one can own any part of a river:

not the water, not the bottom, not the fish, not the weeds." I kicked a rock and barked, "Rivers are public property!"

Emmett is a patient man, so he let me carry on until I finally settled down, then he took the opportunity to tell me about property rights in the western states. He explained that rivers are public in the West, just as they are in the north central part of the country or back East. "However," he explained, "there is one important difference. Riverbeds are often private out here in the Rockies. Since the water is public you can float the river in a boat, but you can't even put an anchor down, not when the riverbed is privately owned." I must have been struck with a bewildered look because Em simplified the story further. He said, "We own the water. They own the ground. You see?"

I understood the law conceptually. Nevertheless, my mind was still wrestling with the image of a boat full of fly-fishers floating public water but unable to drop their anchor because the rocks on the bottom belonged to somebody. I said, "It must have taken some wrangling to convince an entire state full of people that they can't touch the rocks on the bottoms of their own rivers."

Em explained that Wyoming's water laws were written at a time when most citizens were major landowners. Property rights were seen as sacred, and the concerns of ranchers and miners trumped the public interest every time the legislative pen was put to paper. Today, Wyoming is no different than any other state. Few of us are cattle barons or oil moguls.

We're a bunch of worker bees. Wal-Mart is our largest private sector employer, and most Wyoming citizens rely on public land and water for their outdoor sports and hobbies.

I asked, "Do you mean workaday Joes like you and me are living with a set of laws written in an era of cattle kings and unbridled mining claims?"

He said, "I suppose that's true."

As we talked, I continued kicking rocks and scuffing my feet, but we finally made it to the parking lot anyhow. We drove around the private property up toward the bend, and once we were back on public land, we parked the truck again.

We fished the bend until noon, and it was pleasant. I've always believed that rivers are at their best when they're meandering. The temperature was right at seventy degrees, and the wind was light from the northwest. The bend in the river was a nice place to fish. We got skunked there too.

I asked, "Should we call it a day?"

Em said, "I guess we did all we could do."

On our way home, I started thinking about other places where I'd run into NO TRESPASSING signs in the area. I started naming sites where I'd seen similar markers. I said, "I've seen signs at Conner's landing, they surround the Guess Who Ranch, and I've also seen them posted on the Settler's Route." Then I added, "There are PRIVATE PROPERTY signs all over the North Platte."

Em chided me. "Do you think people stand next to the parking lots on the river, whipping the water to a froth in front of their pickups, because those are the best spots to fish?"

I let a pause still the air, then admitted, "I thought those were the best fishing spots."

"Chad. Hello? Those are the only places where we can access the water. The rest is private. The only way you can even pass through is in a boat."

We changed the subject. My world had just become a smaller place.

Lynn was waiting in the yard when we drove up the driveway at home.

"How'd you do?" she asked.

"Not so good," I said.

"Skunked?"

"Yeah. Skunked."

"Oh, well. You'll catch one next time."

"I suppose."

I said good-bye to Em and sulked into the house. I grabbed a beer from the fridge, sat down at our dining room table, and gazed out the window at the traffic on Thirteenth. My eyes panned the front lawn, and I noticed the grass was dry. It also occurred to me that the chokecherry trees needed pruning. Then the sidewalk caught my attention.

Our front yard has a stripe. The stripe is a public sidewalk running across our private property. My mind stopped on that thought, and my brow must have wrinkled into an unlikely furrow because Lynn walked in and asked, "What?"

I said, "Oh, nothing. The front lawn is just a little dry. That's all." Then I spilled my guts.

I told Lynn about our run-in with the NO TRESPASSING signs on the river. I described the other signs I'd seen on the North Platte, and I told her what I'd learned about Wyoming's water laws. She listened with a modest level of interest while I talked about my fishing trip, but she perked up when my thoughts turned back to the yard. I said, "Now, look what we have here. Everywhere I go I'm kept off the river by private property owners, but here in my own yard I have a sidewalk serving as an invitation to trespass. We're practically inviting people to walk across our land."

"That's it," I said, "I'm making some signs." Because we have two cats I decided we would call our downtown bungalow "Dos Gatos Ranch." I told Lynn, "I'm going to make signs that say KEEP OUT, NO TRESPASSING, PROPERTY OF DOS GATOS RANCH, VIOLATORS WILL BE PROSECUTED," and I added, "I'm going to put them all along the sidewalk."

"Oh-no-you're-not," she replied.

I said, "Come on, Lynn. We're not in Wisconsin anymore. This is the West. We have to quit thinking—open hearts, open minds, open doors. We have to protect what's ours. We need to keep the riffraff out. We need to turn our two bedroom rambler into a fortress."

"Finish your beer. Then turn the sprinkler on."

"All right."

My wife has a nice way of putting me on track whenever I go over the top. I walked outside to get the sprinkler, but I took an extra minute to look for a roll of poster-sized paper we had stored in the garage. I was thinking the paper would make a nice NO TRESPASSING sign.

I started rummaging through a pile of items we no longer keep in the house. I pulled a VCR off the stack, sifted through a bevy of racquets, lifted the lid off of a storage bin, and peered down into a loose collection of hockey pads and discarded bicycle parts. Then, unsatisfied, I let the lid fall back on the box.

But a flicker of light caught my attention before the top settled on the bin. There was a glimmer of something inside, a shine coming off a piece of glass. It was the sun reflected in my old diving mask. I pulled it out of the box, and a flashbulb went off in my head.

I recalled Em's explanation of Wyoming water law: the rivers are public, but the rocks on the bottom are often private property. I remembered that it's OK for a boat to float on the surface as long as it doesn't make contact with the riverbed. Then I thought, "What about me?" I wondered if it would be all right if *I* floated on top of the water as long as *I* didn't touch the riverbed.

I don't have a legal mind, so I can't always see the implications of my actions, but in this case I couldn't see how anyone could keep me from snorkeling the river. I'd come to believe I could be kept from wading, but I was sure that I had a right to swim the North Platte. Unfortunately, it was too late in the day to test my hypothesis. My scheme would have to marinate overnight.

My experience in waders taught me that the water would be too cold for swimming trunks alone, so in the morning I stopped at the local scuba shop and rented a wetsuit. The clerk handed me a suit and guaranteed that it would keep me warm, even in the ice cold waters of the North Platte River in the fall. Twelve dollars later, I was driving down the highway toward my first snorkeling trip in a decade.

My first stop was the Golden Goose Ranch. I'd bumped into its KEEP OUT signs several times, and I knew they stood between me and a promising fishing hole. I parked the truck at the public access point adjacent to the Goose and stared down into the water moving by me on the bank. There were serious shadows ghosting around at the bottom. This would be a good day to fish. Large trout were holding in the pools, but I didn't even have a fly rod with me—just a wetsuit, mask, snorkel, and a long pair of fins.

I forgot how awkward it is trying to walk in flippers. I took it slowly, one foot after the other, and when I made it to the river I walked in up to my waist. I shivered for a minute, because the water was awfully cold, but eventually I dropped all the way down into the Platte. I was probably a sight—eyes bulging, arms and legs flailing. After fifteen minutes the suit was fully soaked. The water inside came up to a comfortable temperature, and I finally relaxed enough to make progress. But the current was stronger than it looked.

I tried to make my way upstream off public land and onto the Golden Goose, but it was tough, it took all the energy

I had. It was worth it, though. At one point I looked up and saw a KEEP OUT sign moving by on the left. "I'm in," I thought to myself, and in that moment I was struck by a unique sense of satisfaction, the kind that can only be derived from an act of pure mischief.

I continued upstream for half an hour, but it was taxing. I resorted to rolling over on my back, because I made better headway like that, and eventually I passed a house onshore where there happened to be a man out working in his yard. He saw me kicking like mad, and it didn't take any time for his benign gaze to turn into a long, disapproving glare. I stared back at him through the glass in my mask, smiled without taking the snorkel out of my mouth, and waved. He didn't find any humor in my presence on what he thought was his own personal piece of the North Platte.

Five minutes later I thought, "OK. I made my point. I've flouted my home state's public statutes, and even offended a landowner. That's enough for one day." I turned around, flipped back onto my belly, and started the drift downstream.

Floating along with the current was different. It was easy. I relaxed, the water carried me, and with my mask pointed toward the bottom, I could see the features of the riverbed: logs, rocks, tires, plants, and trout! I caught them off guard. They scrambled as soon as they saw me, but I definitely made out the shapes of two frantic rainbows. I started thinking, "This could be fun." I was a trout voyeur. I kept as quiet as I could and let the river do all the work. I wanted to create the outward appearance that I was a fallen tree or some other form of debris cast down from above (never mind the snorkel and mask). My strategy worked. I didn't get too close to any trout. They are excitable, as you know. But I caught several fleeting glances on my way back to the truck.

I'll admit, my original interest in snorkeling the Platte was born out of an attempt to undermine the property rights of several Wyoming ranchers, but by the time I made it to the truck, I was really enjoying myself. I made a sport out of sneaking up on fish, even if it was just to catch a glimpse of their tails swishing or their sides flashing. I thought, "Swimming with trout—not a bad idea." People have been swimming with dolphins for years, and I always thought that was odd, but swimming with trout actually sounded reasonable. Trout are pretty, they're colorful, and in fresh water you are at the top of the food chain. You can swim with trout all day long and never run the risk of being eaten by sharks. I went home and told Lynn how I snorkeled with trout. She thought I'd been fly-fishing, and when I explained my new technique for chasing rainbows, she said, "Chad, I give up."

In the past, when I gazed upon a stream my eyes panned the water for likely spots to cast flies. Now my eyes were screening for good snorkeling sites, and there was one in particular I wanted to try. Gray Reef Dam. It's the most heavily visited international fishing hole in the region. Big rainbows love the cold water that tumbles out of the gate at Gray Reef, and as a consequence anglers come from all over the world to try their hand at the base of the concrete cork in the river. Every summer the scene looks like an outdoor Jimmy Buffet show. There are RVs, campfires, circus tents, and a mob of trout fans milling around in hats with atypical bills.

I drove out to Gray Reef on a Saturday afternoon and found a place to park among the pickup trucks. I brought my gear down to the river, stood on the bank, and started suiting up. The sight of a man wriggling into a wetsuit was a source of curiosity for the anglers onshore, so when I eased into the water I did so under scrutiny.

As usual, the water was cold and I flinched as a reflex, but this time I was also struck by a rare entrepreneurial impulse. I started thinking, "I could change the nature of this scene." I wished I still had my 1968 Volkswagen Microbus. I thought, "If I still had the bus I could use it to haul masks and fins out to Gray Reef. I could rent equipment to the tourists who come here to fish." I thought, "If I still had the van, I could even paint a slogan on the back: STOP FIGHTING THE FISH YOU LOVE— SWIM WITH THE TROUT." I started thinking I was about to change the relationship between human beings and salmonids. Then somebody threw a rock.

It was a good-sized rock. I'm sure it wasn't meant to hit me. It landed wide by two or three yards, but it felt like a depth charge. With my ears underwater I heard it hit the surface in a crash that sounded explosive.

I stood up and a man onshore hollered, "Hey, get the hell out of there." A fly caster standing knee-deep in the river added, "He's one of those Greenpeace freaks." I scanned the shore left and right. It was elbow-to-elbow on both banks and all eyes were on the man in the wetsuit. An army of anglers was staring my way, and every one of them thought I was about to run interference for the trout below the dam. I backed downstream a few paces and sank underwater. I hung motionless below the surface and let the current carry me away.

I climbed onto shore a safe distance downstream, took off my wetsuit, and snuck over to the truck. I managed to avoid the angry horde, but I started thinking I'd better stick to less popular places, at least until swimming with trout catches on as a sport.

On the drive home, it dawned on me that Barr Creek might be a good place to swim with trout in peace. Barr Creek cuts down through the top of the Laramie Range before it pours onto the plains outside of Casper. It's hard to reach. It takes a major hike to get to the headwaters where trout are found, and the trout are small anyhow. Still, the water is clear and the scenery is worth the effort it takes to get there. All the same, I didn't feel like lugging a waterlogged wetsuit out of Barr Creek Canyon at dusk, so I made it a minimalist trip. I packed a lunch, a snorkel, a mask, a good pair of sandals, and by noon I was standing onshore.

Barr Creek is pocket water. The stream is a series of plunge pools separated by shallow rapids and short waterfalls. I decided to try the pool that greets hikers where the trail meets the shore, but from the bank I could tell creek diving was going to be different. In the North Platte, trout grow oblivious to threats because they're protected by the river's depth and opacity. By contrast, Barr Creek offers fish no protection at all. The water is shallow and clean, and as a result, the trout are skittish. Even so, I saw two trout swimming in place at the top of the pool.

I reckoned, "The only way I'm going to swim with these fish is to sneak up behind them." I walked over to the far end of the pool and donned my mask. I slipped into the creek as quietly as I could, although I had to keep from crying out. The water was cold. Without the benefit of a wetsuit I could tell I was going to be swimming in short bursts.

I crawled forward with my hands on the streambed. The rocks on the bottom were like rungs on a ladder. I pulled myself through the pool, but the water grew deeper as I moved upstream, and eventually I was floating. From then on, I made headway with my hands in a clumsy breaststroke. I moved slowly, and the fish came into view. It was like a game. I wanted to see how close I could get.

Three minutes later, I was looking at the tails of two rainbows. For a moment it felt like I was within arm's reach. I gave a kick and thrust my hand out toward them, but my gesture sent an unnatural wave through the pool and the fish disappeared. My cover was blown.

I climbed back onto the bank. After a while the sun warmed me up to the point where I could sit without shivering, and when I was comfortable enough to move again I crept upstream. I was stalking trout, and the next pool looked like a winner. It was deep, and there was a waterfall at the top.

I had a feeling I'd find trout in pool number two because waterfalls are smorgasbords for fish. The vertical flow washes insects right down past their snouts, and no trout can resist a free meal. I stepped into the water—slowly. I made every effort to keep from jostling the surface. I didn't want to give the fish a clue about my presence in their pool. The plan worked. A school of five trout came into view as I edged toward the waterfall. They were big for Barr Creek. They were browns and each one was longer than a foot.

I stopped because I was trying to be extra careful this time. I was somewhat less than cautious in the previous pool, and I came within inches of an unsuspecting trout. This time I was going to count coup.

Counting coup is a Native American tradition. The Plains Indians were especially attuned to the concept of bravery. In fact, they had elaborate systems in place to measure valor, and the single most meaningful measure was the counting of coup—the touching of one's enemies. To touch a member of another tribe without their consent was considered the highest level of courage and accomplishment. I didn't consider the trout in front of me "enemies," but I imagined that touching one of them was going to take all the skill and patience I could muster.

I inched toward the fish. This time I kept my feet still. I held my right hand behind me and waved it just enough to